Chakra Meditation and Yoga

An Essential Guide to Awakening, Balancing, and Healing Chakras

© Copyright 2023 - All rights reserved.

The content contained within this book may not be reproduced, duplicated, or transmitted without direct written permission from the author or the publisher.

Under no circumstances will any blame or legal responsibility be held against the publisher, or author, for any damages, reparation, or monetary loss due to the information contained within this book, either directly or indirectly.

Legal Notice:

This book is copyright protected. It is only for personal use. You cannot amend, distribute, sell, use, quote, or paraphrase any part, or the content within this book, without the consent of the author or publisher.

Disclaimer Notice:

Please note the information contained within this document is for educational and entertainment purposes only. All effort has been executed to present accurate, up-to-date, reliable, and complete information. No warranties of any kind are declared or implied. Readers acknowledge that the author is not engaging in the rendering of legal, financial, medical, or professional advice. The content within this book has been derived from various sources. Please consult a licensed professional before attempting any techniques outlined in this book.

By reading this document, the reader agrees that under no circumstances is the author responsible for any losses, direct or indirect, that are incurred as a result of the use of the information contained within this document, including, but not limited to, errors, omissions, or inaccuracies.

Your Free Gift
(only available for a limited time)

Thanks for getting this book! If you want to learn more about various spirituality topics, then join Mari Silva's community and get a free guided meditation MP3 for awakening your third eye. This guided meditation mp3 is designed to open and strengthen ones third eye so you can experience a higher state of consciousness. Simply visit the link below the image to get started.

https://spiritualityspot.com/meditation

Table of Contents

PART 1: CHAKRA MEDITATION 1
    INTRODUCTION 2
    CHAPTER 1: UNDERSTANDING THE CHAKRAS 4
    CHAPTER 2: MEDITATION BASICS.. 14
    CHAPTER 3: HEALING THE ROOT CHAKRA 25
    CHAPTER 4: HEALING THE SACRAL CHAKRA 36
    CHAPTER 5: HEALING THE SOLAR PLEXUS CHAKRA 45
    CHAPTER 6: HEALING THE HEART CHAKRA 54
    CHAPTER 7: HEALING THE THROAT CHAKRA 65
    CHAPTER 8: HEALING THE THIRD EYE CHAKRA 75
    CHAPTER 9: HEALING THE CROWN CHAKRA 86
    CHAPTER 10: YOUR CHAKRA BALANCING ROUTINE 96
    EXTRA: QUICK QUIZ – WHICH OF MY CHAKRAS ARE OUT OF BALANCE? 112

PART 2: CHAKRA YOGA 116
    INTRODUCTION 117
    CHAPTER 1: WHAT ARE THE CHAKRAS?.................................... 119
    CHAPTER 2: INTRODUCTION TO CHAKRA YOGA 126
    CHAPTER 3: GROUND YOUR ROOT CHAKRA 136
    CHAPTER 4: UNBLOCK YOUR SACRAL CHAKRA 149
    CHAPTER 5: BALANCE YOUR SOLAR PLEXUS CHAKRA........ 162
    CHAPTER 6: HEAL YOUR HEART CHAKRA................................ 176

CHAPTER 7: CLEAR YOUR THROAT CHAKRA 188
CHAPTER 8: OPEN YOUR THIRD EYE CHAKRA 201
CHAPTER 9: AWAKEN THE CROWN CHAKRA 215
CHAPTER 10: DAILY YOGA ROUTINE FOR ALL CHAKRAS 227
EXTRA: QUIZ – WHICH OF MY CHAKRAS NEED YOGA BALANCING? 243
CONCLUSION 252
HERE'S ANOTHER BOOK BY MARI SILVA THAT YOU MIGHT LIKE 254
YOUR FREE GIFT (ONLY AVAILABLE FOR A LIMITED TIME) 255
REFERENCES 256

Part 1: Chakra Meditation

A Guide to Balancing, Awakening, and Healing Your Chakras

Introduction

The concept of chakras has taken the world by storm, and for a good reason. Whether it's some character in a TV show thumbing their nose at the idea, or an online guru promising to unblock your svadhisthana (huh?!) for a chunky chump of change, you've likely heard some talk about these amazing energy wheels that we all have within us. The trouble is that most people don't have a clear grasp of what chakras are and only have "surface" knowledge, which means they cannot fully develop their energetic and subtle selves.

Well, dear reader, you're about to step outside of the class of the "uninitiated" and learn so much more than you ever imagined about the wonderful world of chakras. You'll learn all about various forms of meditation that can help you open your chakras and get the energy flowing in a balanced, regular way. This matters more than you may realize because this energy flow sustains all aspects of our lives - physically, mentally, and emotionally. This book will help you make up your mind to implement what you learn as you go along, as it's incredibly comprehensive and does a great job of breaking down all the complex "woo" stuff, making it practical and actionable for you. You'll get a boatload of information on chakras and meditation, but the best part is you're not going to feel overwhelmed with it all. You'll be very eager to go through all the information, turning page after page as you find a lot to learn and a lot that you resonate with.

So, here's the key if you want to make the most of this: Drop all your preconceived notions and hang-ups right here, at the very end of this introduction. Keep your mind open, and think of yourself as a sponge, soaking up all you can. You'll find that some things will draw your attention more than others — don't ignore that. Your spirit knows what you need and what will serve you best at the moment. So, take notes along the way, feel free to revisit chapters, and *take some more notes!* Repetition is how you learn. If there's anything you learn here that you find challenging, the absolute last thing you should do is beat yourself up. Go easy; there's no competition. Maintaining a balanced chakra system is a lifelong one, so go easy on yourself and, most importantly, have fun with it. So, if you're ready, ditch all your baggage here and get ready for a wild, life-changing, energy ride.

Chapter 1: Understanding the Chakras

The chakras represent an ancient Hindu belief system that dates back several thousand years. This system is based upon the concept of a living force, or life energy, called prana (from the Sanskrit word meaning wind). This life energy circulates throughout a person's body and is held in place by hundreds of energy centers called chakras. Along the spine, seven major chakras or energy centers act as a relay station for prana to flow from the diaphragm up through each major organ and into these chakras.

Considered the center of our physical being, each chakra also represents the center of all consciousness. It is also the source of our identity and originates in that central being. When we go inwards, we can align that energy field to see what lies at this very core within us.

Speculations

Some say that the knowledge of chakras originated with Buddha, and others say Hinduism created them to teach people about spiritual evolution. In contrast, others believe that chakras are present in all religions in some form. They're one of many beliefs about the human spirit, a topic fully subject to religious debate for centuries. Different religions have different perspectives on what these centers do, but most agree on their importance when it comes to self-awareness, spirituality, and health.

Why do we have them? According to some, they simply exist to help keep our bodies aligned. Others say they are a way to connect with the divine. In contrast, others see chakras as a way to describe the seven heavenly bodies and the nine levels of consciousness. For example, there's an idea that every person has three chakras, said to represent the three-in-one God or Oneness; others say they are seven, representing the seven heavens. In Hinduism, chakras are also a way of explaining what goes on in our bodies through the process of reincarnation.

What do they look like? While every religion has its version of what chakras look like, they all agree that they are some form of energy. While some say they look like a lotus flower with petals and different colored spots inside, others are almost more like a bubble. Some religions even say chakras are located within your body, while others believe that the chakra itself is an energy field around your body. Each one is said to be connected to a different vital organ, but other than that, all spiritual cultures describe chakras differently.

Where are they found? The chakra system can differ from religion, culture, and tradition. In one, the seven chakras are all in the same place and flow in the same direction; in another, there are nine, and they flow opposite to each other; some say there are ten or twelve. While most of them agree on the number of chakras that exist and their purpose and function, they differ drastically on how many exist at each location.

Do chakras have anything to do with eating? Some believe that it's important to eat foods aligned with our chakras. Things like water, beans, and leafy greens are said to water our third eye, while meat and alcohol are meant for our root chakra. It's said that the foods we eat influence the way we think, feel, and act and thus produce different chakra vibrations or different levels of consciousness.

Do they affect how we behave? Again, opinions differ. Some believe that they give off different energies that affect how we think, while others say they affect our health and mood. These perspectives can vary depending on what you need to learn in life. Some cultures even say that each chakra is tied to a particular faith; opening these channels allows you to truly believe and follow that religion.

What do they do? Most religions agree that chakras are like an antenna, receiving and emitting energy. Chakras are said to receive intuitive messages from the mother goddess or God, which help hold it together or tell us how to evolve. They are also believed to have the power to tap into our subconscious. Some say they receive energy from various planets, while others say that your chakras receive energy from God or Mother Earth when you center yourself. They're usually said to send messages upward toward the pineal gland, which is thought to be the highest control center in the human body.

What do they have to do with auras? Some believe that auras are made up of chakra energy and that when there's an imbalance, one's aura may be affected. This is sometimes used to explain why some people feel more positive or negative than others.

Chakras are a set of seven psychic centers in the human body. The word chakra means "wheel" or "circle" and refers to the point where prana energy — life itself — is supposed to be concentrated. Hinduism holds that there are seven chakras located around the organs of the physical body and that these allow different kinds of energies to be emitted from each organ.

In Hinduism, chakras are centers of energy that release their energy based on the body's needs and beliefs. Moving these energy centers allows one to make changes within their constitution. Each chakra serves a specific purpose. For this book, we will focus on the system with seven major energy centers:

- The root chakra or Muladhara (*Mula* means "root," *adhara* means "base" or "support."

Root chakra symbol.
Mirzolot2, CC BY-SA 3.0 https://creativecommons.org/licenses/by-sa/3.0 via Wikimedia Commons: https://commons.wikimedia.org/wiki/File:Muladhara.svg

- The sacral chakra or svadhisthana (Sva means "one's home," adhisthana means "home" or "dwelling place."

Sacral chakra symbol.
Atarax42, CC0, via Wikimedia Commons:
https://commons.wikimedia.org/wiki/File:Chakra2.svg

- The solar plexus chakra or Manipura (*Mani* means "gem," *puri* or *pura* means "city.")

Solar plexus chakra.
Wikipedia:User:AndyKali, modified by User:Iṣṭa Devatā, CC BY-SA 3.0
https://creativecommons.org/licenses/by-sa/3.0 via Wikimedia Commons:
https://commons.wikimedia.org/wiki/File:Recorrected_manipura.png

- The heart chakra or Anahata (This means "unbeaten" or "unhurt.")

Heart chakra symbol.
Atarax42, CC0, via Wikimedia Commons:
https://commons.wikimedia.org/wiki/File:Chakra4.svg

- The throat chakra or vishuddha (Also called *vishuddhi*. Shuddhi means "pure," and vi is a word to represent an intensification of what it qualifies, so vishuddha means "very pure."

Throat chakra symbol.
Mirzolot2, CC BY-SA 3.0 https://creativecommons.org/licenses/by-sa/3.0 via Wikimedia Commons: https://commons.wikimedia.org/wiki/File:Vishuddha_blue.svg

- The third eye chakra or Ajna (Meaning "beyond wisdom," "commanding," or "perception.")

Third eye chakra.
Atarax42, CC0, via Wikimedia Commons:
https://commons.wikimedia.org/wiki/File:Chakra6.svg

- The crown chakra or Sahasrara (Meaning "thousand petals)

Crown chakra symbol.
Atarax42, CC0, via Wikimedia Commons:
https://commons.wikimedia.org/wiki/File:Chakra7.svg

The Purpose of Chakras

The chakra system is an ancient concept that has drawn the attention of many psychics, researchers, and medical professionals. It is considered the center of energy responsible for every human function — from reproduction and digestion to emotions and thoughts. Each chakra serves as an energy hub, passing information from the body and mind to other brain parts.

Chakras are an integral part of spirituality, emphasizing balancing one's energies throughout life. Chakras are located along the length of the spine, starting at its base level with our first or root chakra. These chakras govern our basic survival instincts and physical functions, such as digestion and communication with the upper brain.

More than anything else, the chakras are thought to be spiritual and energetic centers. Their role in a person's life is believed to be deeper than just physical, for they govern their thoughts, emotions, and actions. Because of chakras, you have access to prana, which is the life force that is thought to play a part in all human actions. When the chakras are working properly, they should supply the body and mind with all it needs to function on a balanced level.

While chakras are an important part of Hinduism, this belief system does not claim exclusivity over the concept. There is an entire field of study dedicated to studying chakra systems and their role in human health and awareness. This area is called chakra science. Today, many people are exploring ancient spiritual beliefs like chakras and modern scientific theories. Theories range from chi energy because of electromagnetic reactions in the brain to internal balancing systems that help -regulate our bodily functions and emotions.

Chakras were used in ancient India as a method of meditation and healing throughout all of life, from childhood to old age. Through meditation and worship of deity forms (Ishta Deva), by practicing karma yoga, samyama yoga or dharma yoga (right action), prayer or bhakti-yoga (devotion through the chanting of mantra), and by performing austerities such as kriya yoga (right action) a person can bring their chakras into balance to function properly within the world.

To better understand the chakra system, it will be helpful to imagine the physical body as the home of your energy body, which houses the chakras and acts as the center of all life energy you have access to. These energy pockets are in the seven chakras found along the spine, starting at the tailbone and moving upward toward the brain. When they are all in balance, it is thought that a person will be happy and harmonious, both within themselves and with the world around them. When one or more of these centers is out of balance (or blocked), then there can be disruptions in our energies with terrible consequences.

Why You Should Open and Balance Your Chakras

We experience various emotions and events throughout our lives that can block or unbalance our chakras. These blocks in the energy flow through the chakra system can create feelings of physical and emotional pain, so it's important to identify these blockages and unblock them as soon as possible.

In addition, chakras play a significant role in the spiritual and physical health of the body. When chakras are open and active, energy moves freely throughout the body, reducing stress and promoting relaxation. Disease symptoms such as headaches, back pain, and poor sleep will often clear when a chakra becomes balanced. By focusing on opening and balancing the energy of the chakra system, you can foster a healthier and happier environment in your body.

If your chakras aren't functioning properly, it's important to identify why this is happening so that you can start taking action to restore balance to your energy flow. Following are five possible reasons for chakra imbalance and how each can be changed to bring about feeling good.

Discomfort: When your chakras are blocked, energy is not flowing smoothly through the system. If this is occurring today, consider ways in which you're experiencing pain or discomfort in your body – it may be even what you're doing when you experience these symptoms. By the same token, think of a time when you felt very happy or content. This can help re-establish a happy mood that may naturally flow with more ease. Another simple fix is to aim for three minutes of breathing exercises to help bring about a more balanced mood and increase awareness around discomfort in your body. For those who would prefer a more physical approach, it's also important to consider what posture or position you're sitting in when experiencing discomfort. While some are unavoidable, many cases of physical pain are related to how you're sitting or lying down.

Emotional Shutdown: It's easy to become desensitized to negative emotions. This can make it easy to ignore a present block in the chakras and instead feel the pain of past events or future fears. By focusing on your feelings from the moment you experience discomfort, you can begin to allow feelings of happiness and contentment back into your life. If you're blocking out mental or emotional pain, it could be a good idea to finally face it. You could try writing down what you're feeling and then burning the paper as a way to release the negative energy from your life.

Environmental Stress: Life is busy today, especially if you work outside the home. The world's busyness can cause increased stress through increased activity – ultimately causing chakras to become blocked and unbalanced. If this is occurring today, consider ways in which you can re-balance your life by bringing more balance to your day-to-day activities.

For those who prefer more natural stress relief methods, consider working with nature to de-stress. Breathing exercises and meditation can also help you relieve physical stress by walking and breathing fresh air to alleviate your mental tension. When beginning to heal the chakras, it's important to consider the physical effects of excess or lack of activity and how this affects your state of mind.

Sadness and Depression: Many people today are likely experiencing signs from past lives or past circumstances that seem to repeat in their present lives. These old patterns may still influence you today through a low mood or depression. The tips for releasing emotional shutdowns will apply here as well. By working with your thoughts, you'll be able to change your present situation and resolve negative emotions from the past.

On a physical level, it's important to identify the cause of depression before moving forward. Lack of sleep is one common cause of depression, while poor diet also plays a role. Try creating a healthier meal plan, and don't forget to include the appropriate vitamins needed for proper nutrition.

ADD/ADHD: Before I get into this, please note that this does not replace the actual, professional diagnosis, and you should never self-diagnose. Some people have experienced going from being focused individuals, able to complete tasks with ease, to suddenly unable to focus or concentrate. There are unique circumstances where this could be a chakra block and not actual ADD/ADHD. This happens when you're experiencing "brain fog" – just unable to hold a thought, let alone process it completely. At these times, it's important to realize that you may be experiencing hyperactivity due to increased sensitivity from a blocked chakra. In this case, meditation will help you bring about a more balanced state that will improve your concentration ability. A doctor may recommend medication in addition to changes in lifestyle and diet.

These are only a few basic tips that can help you with your chakras in general. Still, in subsequent chapters, we will focus on each chakra and how meditation can help you awaken inactive ones, balance the overactive and underactive ones, and make sure that the prana continues to flow unimpeded in and through you. Why does this matter, again? You won't have to ask that question when you notice the real effects of this life force flowing in your life, and you'll never need a reminder to always check in with yourself to make sure you're in balance. Now, it's time to talk about meditation.

Chapter 2: Meditation Basics

The meditation process involves disciplining and teaching your mind how to be in the present to enter a state that allows you to transcend the confines of the physical world and access higher consciousness or pure divinity. From this state, you can do whatever you want, whether you manifest something or simply enjoy the rejuvenation that comes from being in tune with spirit – which will automatically pay off in good ways in your physical life. It is absolutely no wonder that meditation has been practiced for thousands of years and continues to hold sway even today. That's because those who make this a daily practice can attest to the many physical and spiritual gifts meditation offers.

Since ancient times, many healing rituals have sought to cure mental illness and increase mental stability. One such ritual used by different cultures throughout time is known as meditation. Meditation has been extensively researched for its benefits in terms of stress relief, improved memory function, enhanced immune system function, increased physical health (particularly heart health), enhanced mood, and reduced anxiety levels.

There are different types of meditation, including Buddhist and Hindu meditative practices and various forms of mindfulness. In any case, regardless of the purpose of meditation, the actual process involves three basic stages:

- A focus on a single point to regulate one's mind
- Breaking through the mental barrier between the observation of external reality and one's mind; and,
- Cultivating an attitude of loving acceptance towards oneself as one is.

The first stage of meditation involves focusing one's attention on a particular object, such as a candle flame or the breath. This regulates the mind by ensuring that it does not stray from its set points. In this way, concentration promotes stable psychological states conducive to meditation. In short, the meditator trains his mind to achieve a solid and lucid focus. This is done through repetitive chanting of a certain mantra, which we'll get into in a different chapter.

The second stage of meditation is known as "breaking through" or "breaking the barrier." The meditator's objective is to clear distractions and focus on one single point during this stage.

The third and final stage is self-acceptance. The meditator now seeks to accept themselves as they are in their present state. The meditator begins to understand that the mind is not separate from the body and that one can feel and think unhindered by any artificial barriers such as walls or thoughts. In this stage, a person comes to accept themselves under all circumstances.

Each level has its benefits and challenges. For example, concentration may lead to a stronger sense of awareness, making one more receptive to the message of meaning contained within practice. On the other hand, concentration also can create a type of "psychic numbing," which may make it difficult to accept oneself and others.

Why You Should Meditate

Why should you even bother to meditate? If you're constantly on the go, with your head in a dizzying array of thoughts and worries, meditation can help. Meditation slows down your brain waves to help you relax and focus. Sure, it's always easy to say "relax" because we all know what it feels like in theory. But when we're running around town all day with barely any time for ourselves, how do we expect to do any deep breathing exercises?

Meditation is a form of hard work for the brain — and there's no better example than syncing up our heart rates with our breath as one long continuous inhalation or exhalation. That scale of work? That's what makes it crucial to have a "go-to" time in our lives that we can dedicate to meditation.

Meditation is a mental exercise. When most people think of exercising, it is in the image of spending hours at the gym with weights and machines. In some sense, meditation is similar— a sustained period of focused energy that tones the mind with considerable benefits. By meditating consistently for five minutes or longer each day, you'll notice an increased sense of calmness and happiness in your life and less stress and chronic pain.

Meditation trains your brain to focus on one thing at a time and ignore distractions. That's one of the most difficult things for people these days, but it's crucial, especially when being productive at work or in school. Meditation is a skill you can develop and master with patience and practice. The more you do it, the easier it will become for you to concentrate and focus, even in difficult situations — like sitting through dull meetings or lectures or sitting through rush hour traffic. You'd be surprised at how stress-free our lives could be if only we could take a few minutes each day to clear our minds and focus on something else entirely.

So why else should you be excited about making meditation a part of your daily routine? It helps with aging and improves your brain's physical health. When your brain waves slow down during meditation, your brain's frontal lobe becomes sharper. At the same time, the left and right hemispheres are synchronized and become more evenly balanced — which allows your mind to operate at its peak energy level. (Nearly all of us fall behind in that area as we age).

Meditation reduces stress and makes you happier. It also helps you learn and focus better. When you meditate, you start noticing changes in your physiology and mind: you begin to build a new memory circuit for learning. You become more attentive and focused over time. It can also create a sense of well-being, a positive feeling that can help improve your health in so many ways, including a stronger immune system. It's no secret that weak immune function can lead to numerous chronic diseases, including heart disease, cancer, and diabetes. The reason? Stress. The less stress you experience, the healthier your immune system will be — which can help prevent these illnesses from lingering in the first place.

Types of Beginner-Friendly Meditation

The Breathing Meditation: The first meditation you should learn is breathing meditation. Breath awareness is the key to meditating, and it's one of the most basic techniques that novice practitioners learn. This basic meditation can be done anytime, anywhere.

1. Find a quiet, comfortable spot where you'll not be disturbed and can relax for anywhere from five to 20 minutes.
2. Sit on a chair or on the floor, whichever feels most comfortable to you.
3. Close your eyes or keep them open with a soft focus. Start focusing on your breathing — as if your breath was physically in front of you as an object that you can see moving in and out of your body with each breath.
4. If you have never done this type of meditation before, you may notice that your mind will wander away from the breath and towards other thoughts or concerns. That's fine — just acknowledge when this happens and gently bring your focus back to your breathing.
5. As you continue meditating, the length of time between distractive thoughts will grow longer, making meditation easier for you during those times when not much else is going on in your life aside from sitting still.

The Body Scan Meditation: If you're new to meditation, learning about each part of your body and how it feels can be very helpful. In this kind of meditation, you'll focus on different parts of your body and feel what they are like. For example, you may concentrate on the muscles in your legs as you tense them up or listen to your heartbeat or the sounds of your breath. You can also focus on things like pressure, temperature, and tingling sensations all over your body.

Journaling Meditation: Not every meditation has to take place inside your mind or in a quiet room with soft lighting. You can also use writing to meditate. This is a great option for those of you who are interested in creating a daily practice but don't have time in your schedule to sit still and meditate — or who need an extra tool that can make meditation part of your routine.

Walking Meditation: Walking meditation is a very different type of meditation that requires becoming aware of each step you take. As I mentioned previously, this is an active form of meditation and not just a regular walk outside in the park. Begin by slowly and deliberately walking— the slower you walk, the better. As you walk, become more aware of each step. What does each step feel like? Are your feet touching the ground on each step you take? Does the weight of your body affect the pressure that every step puts on your feet? How does it feel to take a deep breath and then release it as you put one foot in front of the other? Before long, you'll realize that this kind of meditation is easy to do anywhere at any time, and, in fact, it may become second nature in time.

Yoga: I'm specifically referring to the beginner-friendly form of this practice. Yoga is a great way to start a meditation practice centered on movement. Yoga is a great way to find the balance between body, mind, and spirit. Depending on your yoga practice, you may also find many ways for you to meditate — you can use guided meditations during class or focus inwardly as your body stretches and moves to different poses. You may even feel like experiencing some of the same peace and serenity as in other forms of meditation while on the mat. Many people feel this is a great way to get accustomed to meditation if they do not know how to do it correctly.

Here's a Bonus Way to Meditate: With your senses. Meditating with your senses is another great way to meditate. This involves sitting quietly, identifying, and focusing on different things that you hear, feel, smell, taste, or see. If you can focus on different things, you'll be able to lose your sense of self and become more aware of the world around you. When people practice this type of meditation, they report feeling calmer and more relaxed after they are finished.

If you do not have time for a lengthy meditation session or if it just does not fit into your schedule, consider meditating for five minutes before work or before bed. You can even just close your eyes for five minutes and meditate for a moment before opening them. Even a short meditation is better than no meditation at all.

What Is Chakra Meditation?

Chakra meditation is all about making sure the energy centers or chakras in your energy body remain open, active, and balanced. In this form of meditation, you'll be working with your knowledge of the chakras and how they interact with each other and your body. This is different from just recognizing one's physical body, as we must be more aware of our energy system. So, if you're practicing chakra meditation, you should expect to become more in tune with this other, subtle energy part of yourself.

This is not an easy thing to do, but it is a very helpful technique for eliminating tensions in your life or improving the quality of your life. You may look at the chakras as being similar to musical notes on a musical scale. When something's off, the result is awful discordance. The placement of notes on the scale is important. In the same way, when you're in balance energetically, your energy system is working well, and so do other aspects of your life — and when it's not, your energy is out of alignment.

In chakra meditation, you need to learn the different energy centers of your energy system and how they interact with each aspect of your body and life in general. For example, the first chakra is located at the base of your spine, and it is associated with sexual organs. It is also associated with the emotions and needs of the body. If you've been having issues with these things, you can easily do some root chakra work.

Once you learn the specifications of the different chakras, you can then decide how to work with them. So, for example, if your first chakra is in a disharmonious state and needs to be worked on, then the best thing to do would be to meditate on your body as it is now. If your second chakra is too intense or overactive, then you might want to use breathing techniques like pranayama exercises that can help calm your energy system down and bring it into balance. You'll learn more about working with each chakra in later chapters. For now, let's address the various myths and misconceptions about meditation.

For each chakra, all you must do is work with the breathing meditation but keep your awareness on the chakra you're working with. You can imagine the chakra's color in question enveloping your body or envision the chakra itself as you breathe. You can visualize that the breath you inhale and exhale goes in and out of your chakra instead of your nose or mouth.

Visualizations for Meditation: Necessary or Not?

Visualizations are helpful for meditation if you're not used to meditation and have a hard time getting what you want out of your meditation practice. However, you need to realize that visualization isn't the same thing as meditation — it can work as a helper and training tool. Still, it's up to you to use visualization in a way that prompts your mind into a meditative state.

Visualizations are usually done with your eyes closed while sitting in the lotus position or while lying down (the lotus position is preferred because it helps keep both legs and arms symmetrical). It's important to be in a quiet place where you won't be disturbed to concentrate on the things happening in your visualization. You want to begin this process by closing your eyes and then taking a deep breath in through your nose for four seconds and exhaling through your mouth for eight seconds. Next, find a place where you want to visualize. You can visualize anything from a quiet and peaceful garden to a nice place where the sun is shining brightly. What's important is that you stay focused on what you're visualizing, but if you start to get bored or are having trouble with the visualization, then stop and try again later. One thing to remember is that though visualizations are helpful, they aren't as effective as actual meditation because they aren't as direct.

Debunking Myths about Meditation

There are a lot of misconceptions and myths about meditation. I'll address a few of them here.

Myth #1: Meditation Is Not Religious

Meditation is not inherently religious, but that doesn't mean that it cannot be practiced by those who are religious or spiritual or who have a specific belief structure. Meditation focuses on the practitioner and their experience in the moment, not on any higher power, deity, or other spiritual force that makes the sunrise and set each day (although you're well within your rights to meditate on your preferred deity). Meditation is about learning to connect with yourself deeper than you usually do throughout your day-to-day life, whether or not this is connected to spirituality.

Myth #2: You're Not Doing Anything Important

The thing about meditation is that it's an effective way of doing something important — the thing you do at the end of your meditation when you bring your focus back to the present moment is very important. It can be as simple as calming down and focusing on your breath for a few minutes or something much more elaborate, like creating a positive mindset for yourself or resolving an issue or problem in your life. Something as simple as increasing your life force energy or increasing the quality of your body and mind at the end of meditation is extraordinarily important as it will help all aspects of your life.

Myth #3: Meditation Is Not for Everyone

Meditation is not a fad or a passing trend. It was started thousands of years ago and is still practiced worldwide today, both by religious people and those who follow no particular religion. Meditation is also used in various other ways to help people enhance their lives mentally and physically. You don't need to be a monk who has meditated for 24 hours a day for the past 50 lifetimes. You don't even need to be spiritually inclined. All you need is you and five minutes. That's it. That's about as "for everyone" as meditation is.

Myth #4: You'll Get Uncomfortable

If you're not used to sitting in one place for a long time, you might experience minor physical discomfort. As many people have found, the most difficult thing about beginning a meditation practice is getting used to sitting still for even a few minutes. This doesn't mean that you need to get up and walk around — if you do this, your meditation will be over. You can sit and move your legs every once in a while or give your head or body a light shake in case of discomfort. You'll get used to it after you've done it enough times.

Myth #5: You Need the Perfect Mindset

Meditation is not about putting on rose-colored glasses and thinking, "everything is fine and beautiful." It's about being mindful of your current state at any given moment, from the perspective of that moment and not some fantasy of how things were supposed to be in your life. In other words, if you're looking for an imaginary perfect life where you have everything resolved and don't have any issues or problems, or if you're just looking for something to make your life more enjoyable or make your day go smoother, then meditating is not going to make that happen. Meditation is a process that helps you become more aware of your reality and gives you the tools to deal with life as it is, not turn it into some Pollyanna that doesn't exist.

Body Positions

To keep things simple, you can just sit on a chair with a straight back, feet flat on the floor, and palms comfortably on your thighs. You can also sit in the lotus position, with your legs folded in towards your torso and crossed at the ankles as monks do. You can also meditate in a recliner but be sure that you don't fall asleep. The same applies if you choose to meditate while lying down. It might be helpful to hold up a hand in a position that will cause it to fall if you slip off into sleep. This assumes you're not doing a moving meditation like yoga or walking.

Breathwork

Breathwork, also called pranayama, is a form of meditation that involves using your breath to reach a heightened state of awareness. It can help you develop control over your mind and allow you to "quiet" your mind. The goal is to learn how to be completely present in the moment you're living in and not some fantasy of what the future holds. When done right, breathing can become pleasurable and enjoyable — something that people often say they find relaxing or calming once they've mastered it. You simply breathe in a certain way and then breathe out differently. You keep doing this until you feel that you've calmed your mind enough to go back to feeling like you're awake and alive.

Breathwork is done at different speeds to help with the practice results, but most people find that it becomes more meditative at a slower pace around the rate of one breath in, one breath out. It's important to focus on each breath and its quality. This allows your mind to become more focused and aware of what's happening within yourself. The process can be elevated by taking a deep inhalation and holding it for four or five seconds, then slowly exhaling for about seven seconds before beginning again.

As with meditation, the more you do breathwork, the better you'll become and the more you'll be able to progress. It's a great way to get started with meditation, as it can help ease you into sitting in one place for longer periods and getting used to meditating. Breathwork is all about using your breath to focus on being centered and present with yourself instead of letting your mind wander off. It's being aware of what's happening here and now — not some idealized fantasy world that doesn't exist or some nightmares of what could happen in the future if things don't go your way. Later, you'll learn more about the different forms of breathwork for each chakra.

Quick Quiz: Is Meditation Right for Me?

Answer yes or no to the following questions

1. Do you have an interest in meditation?
2. Are you willing to meditate once or twice a day for at least five to ten minutes?
3. Can you spare a few minutes daily to sit and meditate?
4. Is relaxation an important part of your life?
5. Do you want to enhance your life with the power of meditation?
6. Are you focused on being able to do many things at once, or just one thing at a time?
7. Do you want to be able to use mediation to deal with stress?
8. Are you willing to be open to the idea that meditation is not going to always be easy or change how you're feeling?

9. Are you willing to sit in a quiet place and focus on your breathing and how your body feels for five to ten minutes at least?
10. Can you be open to the idea that your mind may wander while you're meditating, but that's ok?
11. Do you want to make meditation a part of your lifestyle instead of a quick fix?

Total Yes: _____ Total No: _____

If you answered yes to most of these questions, then meditation is for you. If you answered no to more than 4 questions, and it's because you think you can't find time to meditate each day, then here's something a certain wise man once said: "I have so much to accomplish today that I must meditate for two hours instead of one." No, that doesn't mean you need to meditate for literally two hours, but you need meditation more than you think you do. Try a week of practice and see how you feel. Again, you only need five minutes.

Chapter 3: Healing the Root Chakra

Before we get into the nitty-gritty of the root chakra, let's take a quick look at the correspondences of this energy center.

Correspondences

Sanskrit: Muladhara

Meaning: Root support

Color: Red

Seed Sound: Lam

Body Location: Perineum

Element: Earth

Psychological Purpose: Survival

Burden: Fear

What Does the Root Chakra Do and Why Is It Important?

The root chakra is located at the bottom of your body, just above the place where you sit on the floor when you're meditating. It is one of your main "energy centers" and helps you be more grounded, support a healthy, loving relationship with yourself or others, and feel connected to nature. The root chakra makes it possible for us to connect deeply with our bodies to take good care of them, allowing us to have a strong connection to our physical needs.

The root chakra can often require karmic clearing to be balanced, but this does not mean that it's "bad" or "wrong. If your root chakra is imbalanced, you can quite literally expect to have a hard time grounding yourself or having a strong feeling of connection to the earth. You can work around this by making sure that your other chakras are balanced, but it's better to do the work instead of hoping for the best. The root chakra also helps you during meditation because it allows you to be more grounded and aware of what's happening within your body and how you're projecting that onto others.

The root chakra is usually associated with our sense of belonging to the earth and having a deep connection to nature. It also has strong ties to emotions. When your root chakra is balanced, you can experience deeper and more fulfilling emotions and be more connected and grounded with yourself. You can feel more at peace with yourself and your environment and experience a strengthened connection to life itself.

Physical Effects of a Blocked Root Chakra

A blocked root chakra can cause many physical effects, but the most common one is experiencing back pain. This is because when you're grounded to the earth and your connection is blocked, and you can't draw in or ground your energy; it stays within your body and focuses on the problem areas. You might also experience other problems like leg cramps, muscle tension, fatigue and exhaustion, high blood pressure, and more.

It's important to get the chakra balanced before it gets worse because the longer it stays blocked, the greater chance you have of developing problems more serious than just general pain. Your blocked root chakra can start shutting down your energy centers. As a result, you might feel dullness around the soles of your feet, and it can get quite painful. If you're experiencing this, try to get help as soon as possible to clear out the blockage so that you don't continue to lose more energy.

Emotional Effects of a Blocked Root Chakra

If you've got a blocked root chakra and are experiencing emotional problems, you should be able to trace them back through your "energy centers" to this one because that's where it usually starts. You can expect to experience different sorts of problems, ranging from depression and anxiety to not being able to find fulfillment in your relationships or work. You also might have trouble with communication because you cannot express your deeper emotions or even feel they don't exist. Rediscovering our inner emotions is an important part of finding what we're looking for, and sometimes our emotions can block us because we're too afraid of where they could take us.

When you have an energy imbalance in the root chakra, you might feel a little disconnected from yourself, which can cause anxiety, depression, or panic attacks. You might be unable to think clearly with all the blockages, and as a result, you're thinking can become clouded. You may start feeling bad about yourself or that you aren't living life at all. These thoughts can be overwhelming for the mind to try to navigate, and it'll be hard for you to trust anything at all when this happens, which can cause confusion and anxiety. Therefore, it will affect your ability to even walk forward towards what you want.

When your root chakra is blocked, you'll have difficulty feeling grounded and emotionally connected to others. You might have a hard time feeling close to others. You'll feel very detached from what's happening around you or feel like an outsider, like there isn't anyone who understands you. This can cause you to make rash decisions which can sometimes be dangerous. If you're experiencing these problems, it is advisable to get the root chakra cleared out to be at peace with yourself and form relationships with others.

Spiritual Effects of a Blocked Root Chakra

If your root chakra is blocked, you'll have difficulty connecting to anything spiritual because you don't feel like you belong here on earth. You might not be able to experience the presence within yourself that leads to spiritual awakening or progression.

In general, you might experience difficulty with your faith in God or any other force, but it can make it difficult for you to believe in anything at all when it's blocked. You might believe in yourself, but there's no trust within yourself, making it difficult for you to open up completely and get what you want out of life.

You might also experience a lack of motivation or desire to do anything. It can be hard to continue with basic tasks and feel the lack of "fire" within your soul that allows you to really push yourself forward towards what you want. Sometimes this is a temporary feeling, but if an energy blockage causes it, it will likely stay longer than most other symptoms, making your life more difficult.

What Blocks the Root Chakra?

Different things can block your root chakra, but we can break it into three main categories — emotional, physical, and spiritual. The root chakra is connected to all the other chakras, so when you're having trouble with your root chakra, all the other chakras will likely be affected as well.

Emotional blocks can be anything from feeling resentment towards others to just not feeling like you have a sense of belonging. Physical blocks can be caused by unhealthy living habits like smoking or drinking more alcohol than you should; your body literally becomes blocked when this happens, and your energy centers shut down one by one. Spiritual blocks can be created by all kinds of things, like not realizing that you're on a spiritual path or not being ready to connect to God or the universe yet. You don't need to become religious to fix this. You simply need to acknowledge that there is something bigger than you out there and trust the universe or the divine. It doesn't matter what you call this force; acknowledging it is a good step in the right direction.

What Does It Feel Like When Your Root Chakra Is Awake and Balanced?

When your root chakra is in balance, you can find yourself in the here and now, grounded and connected with your body and everything surrounding you. You can feel the power of life within yourself, which allows you to be more confident, creative, spontaneous, and powerful. Your relationships with others are warm and loving, and you're able to deeply express yourself in a way that helps others get to know you better.

You can find excitement in life that can make it easier for you to believe in what you want to do and find a way to do it. You can make stronger and more confident decisions because you're not afraid of how they'll affect you or anyone else around you — and this is a very important part of your energy when things start to get exciting. You'll also begin to feel more secure about your life and experience prosperity and abundance in all you do.

Mantras and Affirmations for Unblocking the Root Chakra

It's always helpful to use mantras and affirmations when working on clearing out your root chakra. It can help you focus your intention, giving you a better chance of banishing the energy blockage keeping you from moving forward.

Here are affirmations you can use:

- "I am safe in knowing that all is well."
- "I am no longer a victim."
- "I trust myself to take the right steps toward my dreams."
- "I honor what I might be required to do to get where I want to be. I honor my higher self, and I honor my soul."
- "I release anything that blocks me from living a life of joy and purpose."
- "Every decision I make is based on my highest thoughts and desires. I am unshackled. I am confident in myself."
- "I trust in myself to do the right thing. I trust in my intuition to guide me."
- "I find the strength within me to move forward when others pull me back. I choose to let go of past mistakes and forgive myself for them. I am beginning again."
- "I no longer feel stuck, but I am not moving too quickly either. I am on a steady path toward my dreams, simply

and with focus."

- "I have a strong sense of who I am, and all of my decisions are made because they work in harmony with this identity I've created for myself. My mind is clear; my life is balanced."

As for mantras, the best one to use when working with this chakra is LAM. You can either chant this out loud or chant it in your mind. To be clear, this isn't pronounced as "lamb" but L-Ah-M. You can sing it in the key to C to make it more effective. Also, you can chant, "Oh."

Crystals and Oils

You should consider working with Carnelian, black obsidian, hematite, ruby, and garnet. You can simply wear these as jewelry or meditate with the rocks in your hand. Also, you can meditate on the color red. As for oils, you can use pineapple, jasmine, geranium, patchouli, camphor, sandalwood, and rose essential oils.

Breathwork for the Root Chakra

The best forms of pranayama for the Muladhara are:

- Cooling breath, also called Sitali pranayama
- Alternate nostril breathing, also called Nadi shodhana

Cooling Breath

1. Sit comfortably in any position you prefer. Let your shoulders relax, keep your stomach soft, and make sure your chin's parallel to the ground and your spine is long and elegant. Gently close your eyes.
2. Inhale and exhale through your nose. Do this thrice as you allow your body and mind to settle into the moment.
3. Purse your lips.
4. Now, if you can, make your tongue form a taco-like shape and let it stick out of your mouth. If you can't do this, you can just keep your lips pursed and open, forming a little circle. Keep your tongue resting against your bottom teeth to form a channel that allows your breath to move through with ease. Alternatively, you can have it resting against your

upper teeth.

5. Inhale through pursed lips slowly, taking your time. Allow your chest and belly to fill with air completely (this is why you have to keep your stomach muscles soft).
6. After your belly and lungs are filled with air, close your mouth and exhale through your nose, taking your time with this process.
7. Do five to ten more repetitions to get the most out of this breathwork. You should do 26 reps in the morning and evening of each session, but you can work your way up to that number if you're not comfortable with doing that many just yet.

Alternate Nostril Breathing

1. Sit comfortably and gently close your eyes. Since you'll be sitting in this spot for some time, you want to have somewhere you can comfortably rest your elbow.
2. Your right middle and index fingers should be bent inward toward your palm. Extend your pinky and ring fingers as well as your thumb.
3. Take that thumb and place it against the right side of your nose as if you want to blow it.
4. Let your ring finger be positioned on the left side of your nose.
5. Take a nice, relaxing breath in and out to get ready for the process.
6. Press your thumb against the right side of your nose, shutting off all breathing in that nostril.
7. Breathe in through the left nostril.
8. With your ring finger, press against the left side of your nose, shutting off airflow in the left nostril.
9. Release the pressure on your right nostril and breathe out.
10. Then breathe in through the right nostril.
11. Close the right nostril again and open the left one. Exhale, then close the left one.

12. Continue to alternate nostrils for ten reps. If you start to get out of breath, please give it a rest and come back to it later.
13. When you notice you're losing focus, focus on counting how long each breath takes you in your mind or pay attention to the pathway of the breath as it moves in and out of you.

Yoga Poses for the Root Chakra

The best poses are:
- The Malasana
- The Uttanasana

The Malasana or Garland Pose

1. Stand with your feet shoulder-width apart.
2. Bend your knees into a squat, with your buttocks close to the ground. You can let your toes turn outward, but not too much because the ideal position is with your feet parallel to each other.
3. Your upper arms go on the insides of your knees, elbows bent, palms clasped as if in prayer.
4. Bring both clasped hands to your heart area, and if you can, touch both thumbs to the breastbone. This should help your chest stay out and up.
5. Make sure you keep pressing your thighs and upper arms into each other to keep all your muscles engaged.
6. Think about your spine and envision it being pulled towards the sky through your crown while you envision your buttocks being drawn to the earth so that you have a straight spine. Your shoulders should be relaxed, not drawn up to your ears.
7. Remain in this position for five reps of inhales and exhales, then come out of the pose by straightening your legs. You can do these three more times or go right into a different pose from there.

The Uttanasana or Standing Forward Bend Pose

Uttanasana pose.
Roberto Busconi at Yoga Mon Amour, CC BY-SA 4.0
https://creativecommons.org/licenses/by-sa/4.0 via Wikimedia Commons:
https://commons.wikimedia.org/wiki/File:Uttanasana_finita_1300px.jpg

1. Stand with your feet together and reach for the sky with both hands.
2. Let both arms come down in a sweeping motion on both sides of your body so that you fold to the floor, bending at the hips.
3. Let your fingers and toes be aligned with each other, and if you're more flexible, you can place your palms on the ground and even press down. If you're not able to reach the floor at all, please use a pair of yoga blocks.
4. There should be a slight bend in your knees. Please don't lock them out.
5. Flex your quads and imagine the muscles stretching upwards. This should engage and open your hamstrings.

6. Allow your weight to settle more towards your front, letting the balls of your feet support you. Check your hips and make sure they're over both ankles.
7. Your head should hang loose with no tension in the shoulders or neck.
8. To come out of this pose, you could either go into a different one or come up by pushing down on your tailbone while hardening your abs as you slowly come back to a standing position.

Root Chakra Meditations

You can do any or a combination of the following for at least five minutes (better if you can hit 10 to 15 minutes) while seated in whatever meditation pose you're comfortable in or while doing yoga. You can chant the LAM mantra or "Oh" repeatedly in your mind.

1. You can choose one or several affirmations to repeat to yourself.
2. You can envision the color red.
3. You can sit in meditation and imagine breathing in vibrant red light on each inhale that goes into your root chakra, which you can envision as a red orb of light. Your visualization may show you splotches of black in red. That's the blockage. So, as you breathe out, imagine the root chakra is your nose and that the black stuff comes out with each exhale. Continue to breathe in the red light until you can see and feel your chakra as clear and active, with no blacker in it.
4. To amplify the power of your meditations, you can use the crystals mentioned already by holding them in your hands or wearing them as jewelry.
5. Apply a drop or two of essential oils on an invisible spot close to your collar, or if you don't react to it, you can place it on your upper lip or just beneath both ears on your jaw.
6. Practice meditative eating with red, natural foods. As you chew and swallow (or sip if you're drinking a juice or

smoothie), imagine and feel the food go down as red light towards your root chakra. Don't rush the food. Consider tomato, red onion, plums, berries, red wine, radish, red pepper, and beet. Protein is good, too.

Chapter 4: Healing the Sacral Chakra

Correspondences

Sanskrit: Svadhisthana
Meaning: Sweetness
Color: Orange
Seed Sound: Vam
Body Location: Sacrum
Element: Water
Psychological Purpose: Desire
Burden: Guilt

What Does the Sacral Chakra Do, and Why Is It Important?

The sacral chakra is located in the sacrum, which is a bone at the bottom of your spine that supports your pelvis. The sacrum isn't part of your brain and spine — but it's connected to both and forms a triangle made up of the two main ones.

When these chakras aren't functioning properly, it can be very difficult to live life as you want to because they're all connected, which means that when one is blocked, it can affect everything else as well. All chakras are important, but the sacral chakra is known as the intermediary between your physical body and your spiritual self.

The sacral chakra is known as the seat of all creativity and imagination because it allows you to create something new and unique in your life. When the sacral chakra is blocked, there's a lack of imagination and creativity within yourself, making it difficult for you to keep up with what you want to do. When this happens, you might start getting stuck in one place or repeating things unnecessarily because there's not enough energy or desire to move forward.

Physical Effects of a Blocked Sacral Chakra

How does a blocked sacral chakra affect your physical health? It can cause you to feel sluggish and uncomfortable. It's often speculated that a blocked sacral chakra can cause infertility problems for men, though this hasn't been proven. When the sacral chakra is blocked, women often have an over-excitement or nervous tension. This could be connected with their menstrual cycles because their womb is located there as part of the sacral chakra. Other health conditions that can impact the blocked sacral chakra include heart problems, urinary tract infections, cystitis, and bladder infections.

Emotional Effects of a Blocked Sacral Chakra

When your sacral chakra is blocked, you'll feel detached from yourself. There may be a feeling of being ungrounded and that you can't be productive or relaxed, no matter how hard you try. Depending on the severity of your blockage, it may even hamper your relationships with others because it may leave you feeling distant from them. There can also be feelings of needing to escape from what's happening in your life because everything feels overwhelming to you — which is why some people might turn to drugs or alcohol as an escape route.

A blocked sacral chakra may also cause a lot of judgmental thoughts, feelings of nervousness or anxiety, feelings of isolation, depression, or just not feeling comfortable in your skin.

Spiritual Effects of a Blocked Sacral Chakra

Your sacral chakra allows you to be creative and imaginative. When the sacral chakra is blocked, it can negatively affect your spiritual connection with others because you don't feel like yourself. There can be feelings of loneliness, confusion, or even depression, which will make you feel even more alone than before.

You may feel that nothing matters anymore in life and that nothing will ever be any good because no creativity or imagination is coming from within. There can also be a feeling of being overly critical of others and thinking everyone else around you is worse than yourself, which isn't something we should put up with either.

What Blocks the Chakra?

Much like every other chakra, if your sacral chakra is blocked, then there's usually a physical cause for this within your body. Some of these include dietary imbalance, stress, anxiety, traditional medical issues such as kidney stones, bladder infections, prolonged illness, or stress from injuries or operations (these can weaken the body, affecting the sacral chakra). Also, bad habits like smoking, drinking alcohol, not getting enough exercise, or consuming unhealthy food can be blamed.

When it comes to the sacral chakra, blockages can also sometimes occur in your mind because of how you perceive yourself and the world around you. Some things that could hold you back from feeling like yourself include poor body image, negative self-talk ("I'm fat," "I'm ugly"), and self-loathing ("Nobody wants to be my friend anymore").

Also, remaining stagnant in life can cause you to feel like you're not going anywhere, which can cause blockages within yourself, perhaps because you don't like the feeling of staying in one place for a long time.

Some emotional causes of blockages in your sacral chakra include anxiety and stress, depression, unhappiness with your current situation and relationships, difficulty at work or school, financial trouble, jealousy, or envy toward others. You could also feel that your chakras are blocked because of disconnection with what spirituality means to you or something you feel guilty about and can't let go of.

What Does It Feel Like When Your Sacral Chakra Is Awake and Balanced?

When your sacral chakra is balanced, you'll feel like everything's coming together in your life, making you feel happy and fulfilled. You'll also be able to create new and exciting things in your life because you're open to them, and they're within reach. This could include starting up a business or discovering some new way of being creative and productive with what you do with your time.

Balance in this chakra usually means there aren't any negative emotions or judgments within yourself, making it easier for you to be around others because they bring out the same feelings within you without causing too much stress. When the sacral chakra is balanced, you'll be able to give and receive love and nurture from others while fully accepting yourself.

You'll be a lot more open to spirituality and will be able to strongly connect with God or your higher power. You'll feel a sense of purpose in life, true self-confidence, and a strong desire to make a difference in the world — without being too overbearing about it either. There'll be a deeper sense of well-being within yourself, which is what we all want in life. We want to feel good about ourselves, and we also want to be able to give and receive love freely without any negative emotions coming up within us.

Mantras and Affirmations for Unblocking the Sacral Chakra

Some different mantras and affirmations can help you clear and unblock your sacral chakra. Try these:

- I am open to all things. I allow them to come into my life with ease.
- I am a loving person, and this allows me to be loved.
- I deserve love and happiness in my life.

- I am grateful for what I have now.
- All is well in my world.
- Ease is the rhythm of life; I let it flow through me freely and easily.
- I am creative, and I allow my mind to take me everywhere.
- I am open to new ideas, thoughts, and possibilities.
- I have a strong sense of purpose in life.
- Everything is working out for me.
- I am free from all blockages within myself and my chakras.
- The universe continues to unfold in exciting ways for me.
- I am an open channel for love and pleasure.
- Spirit flows through me freely, without a price tag.
- I open up to the abundant joy that is within and around me, allowing it to fill my life.
- I am open and receptive to all new loving experiences in life.

Please note that you're free to do so if you feel inspired to say a certain affirmation not mentioned here. Also, note that it's not about the words but the feeling behind them.

As for a mantra, you can chant to clear out your sacral chakra and use the seed sound connected to this energy center: VAM (pronounced V-Ah-M, not like "van"). You can also chant "oo," as in "zoo." To make your chanting more effective, try doing so in the key to D.

Crystals and Oils

The best crystals and stones to use for your sacral chakra to be in balance and active include yellow zircon, Carnelian, coral, amber, and tiger's eye. As for oils, you'll find that bergamot, violet, heliotrope, bitter almond, citronella, orange, and vanilla work well.

Breathwork for the Root Chakra

The best forms of breathwork to bring balance and healthy activity to this chakra are:

- The skull shining breathing technique or Kapalbhati pranayama
- Victorious breath or Ujjayi pranayama

Skull Shining Method

1. Find a nice, quiet place to practice uninterrupted for five to 15 minutes.
2. Make sure you're wearing loose clothing that will allow you to be comfortable during the session.
3. Sit on your yoga mat or a chair in a way that will allow you to be comfortable for the entire session.
4. Allow the backs of your hands to rest on your knees comfortably and let your palms face the ceiling.
5. Keep a straight spine and relaxed shoulders as you slowly close your eyes. Make sure your head is back as well.
6. Move your attention to your belly, and then take a deep breath through both nostrils. You want to breathe in as deep as possible so that your lungs and belly are full of air.
7. As you breathe out through your nostrils, you want to make sure that you're pulling your belly button back as if you're trying to get it as close to your spine as possible. If you do this right, you'll make a hissing noise.
8. Take 20 more breaths in and out to complete an entire session of this breathwork. Keep in mind that the bulk of your effort will be on the out-breaths.

To be clear, this breathing method is not exactly easy when you first start. However, with a few days of practice, you'll sync with your body's natural rhythms, and it will feel easier.

Victorious Breath

1. Find somewhere quiet where you'll not be interrupted for the next five to 15 minutes.

2. Take a seat in a comfortable position and keep your shoulders nice and relaxed. Ensure there is no tension in your neck by keeping your shoulders away from your ears. Gently close your eyes.
3. Bring your attention to the way you're breathing right now. Don't try to change anything.
4. Shift from breathing through your nose to breathing through your mouth instead; inhale and exhale.
5. Now, move your attention to your throat. Pay particular attention to the back of your throat.
6. With each exhale, tense the back of your throat a little bit so that you hear a bit of hissing noise as you breathe out. If it helps, you could pretend that you're Darth Vader or something.
7. After several exhales, you should begin to feel comfortable breathing like this, after which it's time to also tense the back of your throat on the inhales as well.
8. When you become comfortable with inhaling and exhaling this way, it's time to close your mouth and resume breathing with your nose again, still tensing the back of your throat on each inhale and exhale. Do this right, and you should hear a sound with each breath. That's *Ujjayi*.
9. You can incorporate this breathwork (and others) with yoga if you want your sacral chakra to feel extra clear by the end of your session.

Yoga Poses for the Sacral Chakra

The best poses are:
- The dancing goddess, or Utkata konasana
- The bound angle poses or Baddha konasana

The Dancing Goddess

1. Stand on your yoga mat so that your feet are wider than shoulder-width apart.
2. Both feet should be turned outward no more than 45 degrees.

3. Make sure the top of your head is reaching for the sky to have a straight, elegant spine.
4. Slowly and carefully squat. You must make sure your knees are always just above your ankles. Remember that you should exhale as you do this, and you're moving down, not backward.
5. Keep your buttocks slightly tucked into the front, and make sure your thighs are pulling backward. You want the ground and your thighs to be parallel to each other.
6. Check that your spine is straight and relax your shoulders.
7. Bend your arms at the elbows, keeping both palms up and out.
8. Remain in this pose for the next five to ten breaths.
9. To come out of this, just push down into the floor with both feet, and then with an exhale, straighten your legs gently and slowly as you come back to a standing position.

Sacral Chakra Meditations

The meditations are endless in variety because you can mix and match everything you've learned so far, from breathwork to yoga poses, visualizing colors, etc. Remember, you should go for no less than five minutes, and with time you should aim for 15 minutes. You can do the following in whatever position you prefer and can combine them as needed or just pick one thing at a time. (Obviously, you can't do an eating meditation while doing yoga, so while I applaud your ambition, I must caution you against that) You can:

1. Chant the **VAM** mantra or "oo" sound.
2. Pick one or several affirmations to repeat to yourself during your session.
3. Imagine being enveloped all over your body with a brilliant orange glow.
4. As you meditate, envision that you're inhaling brilliant orange light, and that light is going in through your sacral chakra, not your nose. Visualize that chakra as a bright ball of orange energy. You may notice it has black splotches on it; that's fine. Those are the blockages we'll be ridding you

of. So, breathe in bright orange light through your sacral chakra, and as you exhale, see the black splotches leaving through that chakra. Eventually, the chakra should be nothing but pure, beautiful orange energy as you continue breathing. You can pick one of the pranayamas detailed in this chapter to boost this.

5. You can perform your meditations and chant with the crystals we've mentioned before, holding them in your hands as you sit and breathe. You can also wear them as jewelry each day.

6. Use the essential oils mentioned in this chapter as part of your skincare routine or specifically for meditation or breathwork. Please remember to check that you're not allergic to the oil you're using by testing it on the inside of your wrist. You don't need more than a drop or two each time. Putting it beneath both ears on your jaw will allow you to smell it with ease as you do your yoga or meditate. You can also put it on your upper lip or collar.

7. You can do the yoga poses from this chapter while doing your breathwork, pair them with the mantra **VAM** or "oo," or while contemplating your affirmations.

8. Meditative eating is also an option. The foods should be natural, of course. The best foods are rutabaga, apricots, peaches, carrots, pumpkins, eggs, and persimmon. Also, increase your calcium and vitamin A intake if you're not supplementing. As you chew or drink and swallow, just envision the food as orange light and life, moving straight to your sacral chakra to fortify it.

Chapter 5: Healing the Solar Plexus Chakra

Correspondences

Sanskrit: Manipura
Meaning: Luscious gem
Color: Yellow
Seed Sound: Ram
Body Location: Solar plexus
Element: Fire
Psychological Purpose: Will
Burden: Shame

What Does the Solar Plexus Chakra Do and Why Is It Important?

Your solar plexus chakra or Manipura is all about your superego and your subconscious mind. It is a bridge between your body and mind and is located just beneath your ribs, right above your sacral chakra.

This chakra is associated with the element of fire. While we think of this element in terms of the sun or anything flame-related, you must remember that it's not just those things. Fire is also in lightning and forest fires; it lies in anger, love, jealousy, and passion. It even lies within us when we're passionate about something or someone. Think of fire as an intense energy that can either be used for good or bad.

This chakra is critical for your ego, which is a part of you that can take in the outside world and interpret it. This chakra has a lot to do with your ability to learn and study and apply what you learn. It's also very important in terms of doing any physical activity or exercise since it allows you to have the drive and stamina to accomplish what needs to be done. The solar plexus can also help you be aware of other people's moods, thoughts, feelings, and how they might react in different scenarios.

This chakra is important for your emotions as well as it's responsible for helping you control anger and jealousy, as well as love and passion. The more you're into something, the more energy comes from that center, so if you love someone or something very much, this chakra will be working overtime.

Physical Effects of a Blocked Solar Plexus Chakra

If your solar plexus chakra is blocked, you may feel sluggishness – a kind of lack of energy and motivation. You could also experience issues such as constipation or diarrhea, acid reflux, heartburn, stomach pain, indigestion, a weak immune system, or even develop an ulcer. In terms of your respiratory system, if you have breathing issues, you could be dealing with this chakra. You may feel that something is "off" in your body since it's the center of your physical body. Other physical ailments you could suffer are arthritis, back pain, headaches or migraines, asthma, heart palpitations, and anxiety.

Emotional Effects of a Blocked Solar Plexus Chakra

If you think of a blocked solar plexus chakra as only having physical effects on the body, you would be wrong. It also has an emotional effect on us. When it's blocked, we may be unable to express love or get angry at anything. There might also be a lack of confidence or an inability to show affection because the chakra lacks energy. Emotionally speaking, this chakra may make you feel depressed, nervous, or insecure about yourself and your life in general.

On the flip side, if your solar plexus chakra is blocked, you may feel as though your emotions are heightened, but it could also make you extremely jealous or angry. If you're experiencing these kinds of emotions, it could translate into bad relationships and even some risky behavior. You may have difficulty controlling your behavior, and in fact, you may even become violent toward yourself or others in the heat of the moment.

You might also feel defensive or even downright mean when not in control of your emotions. This will lead to problems with relationships and personal interactions at home and at work. You may feel alone in the world.

Spiritual Effects of a Blocked Solar Plexus Chakra

If your solar plexus chakra is blocked, you could have issues with self-esteem and confidence. You may also have feelings of deception or dishonesty. In terms of any spiritual beliefs, you might be more likely to question what really exists . . . and if there really is an unseen force out there, looking out for us. If not rectified, this will lead to an overall feeling of loneliness and confusion in your life.

You may not be able to see the world (or certain individuals) clearly and make good choices. You may feel as though something is always being taken from you or that you're lacking somehow. Financially, you could feel as though it's a struggle to get by or even have enough money for the necessities of life.

What Blocks the Solar Plexus Charka?

There are more than a few physical causes of a blocked solar plexus chakra. Some of the most common are digestive issues and respiratory problems. You might also have a vitamin deficiency, especially if you've been dealing with headaches.

The emotional causes of a blocked solar plexus chakra are very similar to the physical ones. You might have eating disorders or unhealthy dependence on others in your life. You may also be experiencing anxiety or depression, which can lead to self-destructive behaviors. There could be some relationship issues causing you stress, whether at home or work. Being in a situation where you feel like you can't control any aspect of your life will block this chakra.

You may want to look at your spiritual beliefs as well when dealing with a blocked solar plexus chakra. You may have lost your way and are no longer sure what your spiritual belief is. All these things can make you feel isolated, confused, and alone, leading to blocked chakra.

To release this block, you must look at the physical symptoms (which usually tell the story in terms of what kind of energy is lacking), your emotional issues, and spiritual confusion – and find ways to resolve them.

What Does It Feel Like When Your Chakra Is Awake and Balanced?

Having a balanced solar plexus chakra can make you feel good and on top of the game when it comes to getting things done. Your productivity is probably at an all-time high, which is great for anyone who has goals they want to achieve in life. You'll feel happy, secure, and confident when this chakra is balanced.

You'll also have a clear vision of what lies ahead for you and be able to follow through on your goals. If there are any problems, you'll deal with them head-on instead of letting them fester and grow until it's a much larger issue than it needs to be. A balanced solar plexus center can help prevent that from happening.

A balanced solar plexus chakra means that you can still feel the same amount of energy coming from the center of your body, but it doesn't cause you to overreact or get too worked up. You feel as though everything is okay with you regarding your emotions and how they affect others.

When your solar plexus chakra is balanced, you feel like your life has a purpose and that you're in control of it. You feel confident and capable of achieving anything you set your mind to. You can see things clearly and make good choices with a clear mind. Your financial situation is great – or at least improving if it's not where you'd like it to be. Dealing with people is a breeze since you know how to approach them to get what you want out of them or from the situation.

When this chakra is balanced, it's easier to prevent illness or deal with it when it comes up without stressing about it. Your spiritual beliefs are in check, and you know that you have purpose and can control your fate.

Mantras and Affirmations for Unblocking the Chakra

You can use any of the following affirmations:

- I am powerful.
- I will maintain my power even while being sensitive and humble.
- I have no reason to be afraid; I can handle whatever comes up in my life.
- I am healed and whole.
- The power of mastering my energy is within me now.
- I am learning to be self-reliant and loving all the while.
- I am in control of my life situations, my relationships, and myself.
- I am in a safe and secure environment.
- I am prepared for what lies ahead.
- I am safe, secure, and confident in myself.
- I can relax now, knowing that I'm ready for whatever life offers me.
- My health is improving each day.
- My relationships are constructive, beneficial, and honest.
- My spirituality is grounding, and I know that everything is taken care of in the universe.

- I have balance in all areas of my life, including my work and my finances.
- My productivity is high, which helps me reach my goals easily.
- I am at peace with my life, my surroundings, and myself.
- Everything is in place, and I know that it will be okay.
- I can handle anything that comes my way.

As for a good mantra, you can chant it in your mind or aloud during your other solar plexus opening exercises. You can use the seed sound RAM, which is pronounced R-Ah-M, not "ram" like the verb or the animal. You can also chant "ah," and whatever you choose, doing so in the key of E will make it more effective.

Crystals and Oils

You can use amber, citrine, golden topaz, yellow sapphire, and yellow jasper. Citrine is awesome as a gem because it can help with neutralizing negative energy, while amber is great at lifting the spirits. Topaz encourages optimism while helping you work toward what makes your heart sing. As for oils, use orange, lemon, lavender, and rose essential oils.

Breathwork for the Solar Plexus Chakra

The best breathwork to use for your solar plexus chakra is the bumblebee breath or Bhramari pranayama. You're going to love this one because it'll bring instant calm to your mind. However, don't just pull it out to use when you feel frustrated or angry. Make it a practice. Here's how to do it.

The Bumblebee Breath

1. Make sure you're wearing something loose and comfortable.
2. Find a quiet spot where you'll neither be distracted nor bothered for at least five to 15 minutes.
3. Gently close your eyes.
4. Now, you're going to press down on the cartilage of your ears with your forefingers. To be precise, you'll be pressing down on the part that would cover the hole in your ears.

5. Take a deep breath in, and as you exhale, press down on the cartilage while you hum like a bee.
6. Inhale and exhale this way 6 to 7 times, take a breath, and then go again. You can stop when you're done if you've gone on for five minutes and feel like you don't need to continue further.

Yoga Poses for the Solar Plexus Chakra

For yoga poses, you're going to do the following poses:

- The alternate leg raises
- The cobra poses or Bhujangasana

Alternate Leg Raise

1. Wear comfortable clothing, and then lie on a yoga mat on your back with your feet together.
2. Notice the way you feel on the floor. Connect with the earth and allow it to ground you in the present moment as you breathe in through your nose and out through your mouth.
3. When you feel grounded, put your hands on your belly.
4. As you breathe in, allow your fingers to separate from one another, and as you exhale, let them come back together.
5. Raise your legs to the ceiling, and then bend your knees ninety degrees to see your toe tips above both knees.
6. Slowly allow your right leg to go lower, so it hovers just above the floor, and then remain in that position for a few breaths, then bring the leg back to its starting position.
7. Do the same thing on the other side. It helps to make sure that you keep looking at your toes and make sure your hands are palms down on the ground and by your side. Also, flex your feet as you switch them and make sure that you keep your tailbone pressed into the earth for stability.
8. When you've done 10 reps, you can allow your legs to come back to the ground and then stretch out.

Cobra Pose

Cobra pose.
https://www.pexels.com/photo/woman-doing-yoga-pose-4473610/

1. Lie face down on your yoga mat. You want to make sure that your palms are beneath your shoulders and your elbows are bent. Your arms and elbows should be pressed down to the sides of your body.
2. You should make sure that you're looking down at the floor and keep both your spine and neck in a neutral position.
3. Root your hips into the floor to have a solid base to start lifting yourself.
4. Take a deep breath in as you push your palms into the floor and raise your chest off it. Please ensure that your elbows never leave your sides because you'll likely hurt yourself if they do.
5. As your chest is raised, make sure that your spine remains neutral. Hold that pose for a few breaths, and on an exhale, you can lower your chest back to the ground, keeping your elbows to your sides as you do so.

Solar Plexus Meditations

Whatever you decide is worth doing, make sure you take five to 1five minutes, and no less than that. As always, combine these however you feel.

1. Chant **RAM** or Ah in meditation, either in your mind or aloud.
2. Choose whatever affirmations you like and meditate on what they mean, or repeat them just as a mantra during meditation.
3. As you meditate, imagine that there's a bright yellow glow all over your body, coming from the solar plexus chakra. Visualize yourself breathing in bright yellow light through the solar plexus instead of your nose. Imagine the energy center as a bright yellow ball, and if you notice any blotches of black or gray, imagine that the blotches reduce with every exhale as you breathe out the negative energy. Continue until you have a clear, yellow chakra. You can breathe regularly with the breathing technique outlined in the chapter on meditation.
4. Try chanting during your meditation.
5. Use the crystals and oils to supercharge your meditation, or simply wear them each day to help you with this chakra as you go about your business.
6. Perform the yoga poses while focusing on your mantra or affirmation.
7. Meditative eating is also an option here, imagining that the food is a yellow light that goes straight down to your chakra to clean and energize it. Here are good foods for this energy center: Pawpaw (papaya), lemons, yams, pineapples, corn, and natural butter.

Chapter 6: Healing the Heart Chakra

Correspondences

Sanskrit: Anahata
Meaning: Unhurt
Color: Green
Seed Sound: Yam
Body Location: Heart
Element: Air
Psychological Purpose: Love
Burden: Grief

What Does the Heart Chakra Do and Why Is It Important?

The fourth chakra, also known as the heart chakra, is in the middle of your chest. You can find it by placing your hands on your chest near the center. This chakra is important because it controls your emotional well-being, attitude, and how you relate to others, especially when it comes to personal relationships.

The heart chakra controls how we feel emotionally and physically. This chakra plays a huge role in how much effect you have on others, whether you're using your energies for good or ad. If this chakra is blocked, you could be sending out bad vibes which would hinder your life and those around you.

Some of the ways by which the heart chakra is involved in our lives include being able to communicate our emotions, having a positive and loving attitude toward one and all, and expressing love, affection, and trust. Our Anahata is also linked to how we feel physically and how we manage our physical selves. If you're not in good health, it is because you're focusing on your emotions rather than taking care of yourself physically.

Physical Effects of a Blocked Heart Chakra

When your heart chakra is blocked, it causes you to feel isolated and alone, which might make you depressed. You may feel like no one cares about you or that people are purposefully leaving you out. It can cause your physical health to suffer, including your immune system, blood circulation, and breathing. You may begin to have sleeping problems.

If this chakra is blocked for a long time, it can block the rest of your chakras. It's important that you take proper steps to equalize any imbalances within yourself by using the right crystals, essential oils, and lifestyle changes to help unblock your heart chakra. You could also feel as though your heart is pounding out of your chest a little too intensely at times. Your vision may become dark or narrow – like you're looking through a tight tunnel with a light at its end. You may also feel as though you're being smothered by love and kindness around you — too much kindness makes it hard to breathe and you may feel suffocated by opportunities.

These are all physical signs that maybe your heart chakra is experiencing some internal blockage due to a bad outlook on life in general or simply how you've been dealt with over time. You find it hard to trust or love, and you're not open to love either. Someone with a blocked heart chakra may suffer from physical issues with their thymus gland. This gland is responsible for making T cells that fight off microbes and germs and infections in your body. Having a blocked heart center could also lead to inefficient absorption of nutrients from the foods you put into your body, resulting in malnutrition.

Emotional Effects of a Blocked Heart Chakra

You could feel completely incapable about life in general, resulting in severe depression or more serious mental health issues. You'll also have trouble trusting others you meet and get close to and jump to negative conclusions without giving them a chance.

When your heart chakra is blocked, it can cause you to feel alienated, alone, and disconnected from the people around you. You'll feel as though you have no meaning or purpose in life and will lose interest in trying new things. You may also begin to attract people who don't care about you or are not good for you, making your life miserable.

When your heart chakra is blocked or negatively charged, it's hard for others to understand how you feel about things going on around you. It's like trying to communicate with a brick wall when there's no way of getting through it. You'll have a hard time opening up, making it very difficult for people around you to trust you or even want to be around you.

You could feel like no one loves or cares about you, which can lead to feelings of deep depression. You could also constantly feel vulnerable and unable to speak out against what's wrong or right during that particular time in your life.

Spiritual Effects of a Blocked Heart Chakra

When the heart chakra is blocked, it can make you feel like the Universe doesn't want you or care about you. You feel that it hates you and is out to get you, which can be quite painful to endure. Some people experience this when they're going through a difficult time in their lives, such as losing a great friend or finding out that they can no longer have a child.

You may feel as though you're getting punished for something in your past or because of the way some individual has treated you in the past. You could also be overwhelmed by feelings of guilt after learning about someone who has passed away.

If this chakra is blocked, it can cause you to not see the good in life or others. You may begin to lose faith in others around you, making it very difficult for you to trust certain people you come across. You may not be able to find the courage or willpower to be happy for other people's accomplishments. You may also feel as though life has abandoned you and that Divine hasn't done anything for you, which brings about feelings of sorrow and loneliness.

What Blocks the Heart Chakra?

A few things can cause the heart chakra to clog up or get out of balance, especially if you're experiencing stress and anxiety in your life. Things such as bad relationships, divorce or growing apart from people that mean the most to you, serious illness, bereavement, especially related to a parent or relative, heartbreak, or major losses in your life such as loss of a job or important relationship.

You might have been treated unfairly by someone else in your life, which could cause anger and resentment for years. You may also be experiencing some type of abuse in your life from someone else, which include emotional abuse from a loved one or even physical abuse when things are taken too far. Other common causes of a blocked heart chakra are stress, relationship issues, fear of the unknown or uncertainty about things to come, lack of trust in others, yourself, and life itself, overwhelming guilt over mistakes, feeling that you've been wronged, being very materialistic in your outlook on life, having constant thoughts of "me versus them" when dealing with others around you.

There are also several physical events and things that can happen to you during your life that could cause physical blockages. Some of these, as previously mentioned, include smoking cigarettes, drinking alcohol, drug abuse or withdrawal, overeating and obesity, chronic constipation or diarrhea, lack of exercise, and not getting enough sleep.

What Does It Feel Like When Your Heart Chakra Is Awake and Balanced?

When a person's heart chakra is open, they're compassionate people and very giving toward others. They can speak their mind when they need or want to, but there's no feeling of resentment towards anyone. If a person is experiencing a heart chakra that's balanced and awake, they're very supportive of other people in their lives, including family members, friends, and even their significant other. They love to laugh, feel good about themselves, and express themselves without any inhibition.

A balanced heart chakra helps you feel as though nothing can bring you down or keep you from being happy with what's going on in your life at the current time.

If your heart chakra is balanced, you'll feel like someone is always watching over you wherever you go, as though someone loves and cares about you, even when times may be tough for you and you don't think things are working out for the better. You'll feel like the friends that are in your life truly care about your well-being and will do anything to help you if they can.

When this chakra is balanced, you'll have confidence in yourself, your life, and others around you. You won't have any issues with feeling down or low self-esteem when looking at other people that might be better off than yourself. You may also understand what love is when you look at it from different perspectives.

Mantras and Affirmations for Unblocking the Heart Chakra

When you're trying to unblock your heart chakra, you can do a few different things to help it clear faster. Some of these things can include using mantras and affirmations to help you open up the chakra and get everything back where it needs to be. Try using the following mantras or affirmations:

- I love and accept myself just the way I am.
- I'm perfect the way I am.
- My heart feels safe and secure.
- I release myself from the pain that was caused in the past, whether that's recent or long ago. The pain gets released now, allowing me to move forward with my life without any burden on my shoulders.
- I am loved, and I give love back to others freely.

- I know that I am worthy of being loved and that the universe has my best interest at heart.
- I find healthy relationships that are fulfilling to me.
- I feel strong and secure in all types of relationships that I'm in now.
- I am comfortable communicating my feelings about things to people who matter in my life.

As for the mantra, you can either chant Yam (Y-Ah-M) or chant Ay, as in "clay." Do your chanting in the key of F, and you'll have a lot more powerful result.

Crystals and Oils

The best crystals for unblocking your heart chakra include jade, tourmaline, and emerald. As for oils, opt for ginger, benzoin, musk, jonquil, narcissus, tuberose, sage, mint, and lime oils.

Breathwork for the Heart Chakra

You'll need to do the Dirga pranayama for the heart chakra, which is the three-part breath. Here's how:

1. Lie on a yoga mat and close your eyes. Your legs should be stretched out, but if that's not comfortable for you, you can always just bend them at the knees so that your feet are resting flat on the mat. If you opt for the latter position, you should allow your knees to relax against one another.
2. Bring your attention to your body and face and relax the muscles all over.
3. Now, move your attention to your breath. Don't try to change it; just notice it.
4. As you pay attention to your breath, you'll find that your mind may wander to various concerns or other random thoughts. This is fine. When you notice this, simply bring your attention back to the breath as many times as it takes. Please don't beat yourself up for getting distracted, as this will take away from the exercise.
5. Now, take a deep breath through your nose, and breathe out until you're fully emptied of all air.

6. With each inhalation, you want to make sure that your lungs and belly are rising, expanding with air.

7. On the exhales, make sure that you're completely empty, which means that your stomach should flatten out. As you breathe out, please draw in your belly button like you want to connect it to your spine. This way, you can ensure that your stomach and lungs are both empty.

8. Repeat this deep breathing process for five breaths in total, and that's the end of the first part. Now let's move on to part two.

9. On your next breath in, allow your belly to be as full as you can. When you hit the full point, take in some more breath so that you cause your chest to get even wider.

10. As you breathe out, first release the air you've contained in your chest. Do this right, and you'll feel your ribs, once apart, now closing the gap. Then release the air in your stomach by pulling your belly button towards your spine like before.

11. Repeat this new level of deep breathing to do a total of five cycles, and that's the end of the second part. Now it's time for part three.

12. As you take your next breath in, allow your stomach and chest to be full of air. When you're full, gently draw in a little more air to fill the upper chest region, coming all the way up to the area around your collar bone. This will cause your heart center to rise, which is great for activating your heart chakra.

13. As you breathe out, release the air from your upper chest area or heart center first so that it collapses back down. Then release the air in your mid-chest so that the ribs close the gap between them on either side. Then let go of the breath in your belly by pulling the belly button into the spine. Please do this at a comfortable pace for you, so all three parts of this cycle happen seamlessly.

14. Repeat the process for a total of ten breaths.

Please be careful when doing this. The last thing you want to do is breathe so deeply that you feel you're about to rip a lung or something. Also, you want your breathing to be smooth with no straining on your part. If you like, you may practice this while reclining or seated upright.

Yoga Poses for the Heart Chakra

The best yoga poses for the heart chakra are"

- The cat/cow pose or Chakravakasana
- The camel pose or Ustrasana
- The bridge pose or Setu bandha sarvangasana

The Cat/Cow Pose

1. Get on your yoga mat on all fours, with your hands and knees evenly spaced apart from each other and your weight evenly distributed. Think of being a table here. So, your wrists and shoulders should be in alignment, as should your knees and hips.
2. Make sure that your neck is nice and long in neutral spine, your gaze out in front of you. Now let's move on to the cow pose.
3. Steps three to six are to be performed on your inhale. First, bring your attention to your toes. Let their tips rest on the ground, curled under.
4. Next up is your pelvis, which should be tilted back. The effect will be that your rear end moves up towards the ceiling. Think of this move as rippling through your body, from toes to neck, so that the neck moves last.
5. Make sure you're drawing your belly button into the spine even as the belly is pushed towards the floor.
6. As gently as you can, turn up to face the sky, make sure there's no strain on your neck, and it's not at an awkward angle. Now it's time for the cat pose.
7. The following steps are to be performed on the exhale. Move your attention back to your feet and allow their tips to rest on the floor, stretching out at the ankles.
8. Now, tuck in your rear end as you push your pelvis gently forward. Allow this motion to ripple through your body

like the previous pose so that your spine rounds up and out towards the sky.

9. Please check to make sure your belly button is drawn into your spine and your head is leaning to the floor. Think of it like trying to see your belly button.

10. Now it's time to repeat the entire sequence for the next five breaths, or 10 if you feel like a champ and know you can handle it. Remember, inhale the cow, exhale the cat.

11. When you're done with the entire sequence, bring yourself back to the starting position with your spine neutral.

The Camel Pose

1. You'll be kneeling on your mat with your hips over your knees for this pose. If your mat isn't thick enough, you might need to double it by folding it or use something to pad it so your knees feel comfortable. Let the tips of your feet rest flat on the floor.

2. Now it's time to slide both hands up your sides, palms down on your skin, bringing them up to the sides of your chest. Think of it like holding your upper torso with your thumbs on your back and your other fingers on the front of your chest and sides. Your elbows should be sticking out as you hold on to your chest.

3. From this position, open up your chest to the sky by pushing it out and up.

4. Now, with your chest open, move your hands behind you to hold on to your heels. You should move one hand at a time so you don't hurt yourself. If you find that the stretch is too deep for you, simply curly your toes beneath you as you did in the cow pose to have some more height.

5. Pull your hips towards the front, but please ensure they remain over both knees. If you feel comfortable in this position, you can move on to the next step.

6. Allow your head to hang back so that you expose your throat. If you feel this isn't comfortable, you can allow your chin to stay as it was.

7. To come out of this position, first bring back your chin to the chest and then move both hands back to the hips as you tighten your abdominal muscles. You should use your hands to offer your lower back the support needed to return to your initial kneeling position.

Please make sure that as your chest goes back, don't allow your thighs to close together. They're supposed to remain upright, so it's a good idea to do this with your thighs up against a wall to see how you're doing. When doing this pose with the aid of a wall, the idea is both your hips and thighs remain touching throughout the move.

The Bridge Pose

1. Lie down on your mat, feet flat on the ground, knees bent.
2. Reach out with your fingers (your arms should be on the ground) towards both heels. You don't have to touch them, but you should be barely able to connect with them with your fingers.
3. Please make sure your feet stay parallel as you move through this pose, no matter what.
4. Push down into your feet as you raise your hips to the sky.
5. Grab your yoga block and set it just beneath your sacrum at your back; then, you can leave your arms on the ground, still stretched out. If you don't feel comfortable, adjust as needed.
6. Remain in this pose for the next few minutes or as long as you feel comfortable. If you notice your back's beginning to feel pain, come out of the pose.
7. To release this pose, push down into the earth with both feet as you raise your hips to the sky once more. Slide the block out from beneath you and gently come to the ground once more.

Heart Chakra Meditations

Take about five or 15 minutes to do any or a combination of the following meditations:

1. Chant YAM or "ay" in the key to F.

2. Pick one or several of the affirmations given and contemplate on them or say them aloud.
3. Envision a brilliant green light that emanates from your heart center, enveloping you in its glow.
4. Breathe in the bright green light, imagining that it's your heart chakra breathing in and out, not your nose.
5. Picture your chakra as a bright green ball while you sit in meditation, breathing in green light. If you notice some dark energy spots in the chakra, envision them leaving with each exhale, as each inhale energizes and balances your chakra with green light. When you notice the chakra is clear, you may stop if you want.
6. Practice the various breathwork exercises given to you in this chapter.
7. Perform the yoga poses you've been given in this chapter, cycling through them until you hit the five or 15-minute mark, whatever works for you.
8. Use crystals to assist you in your meditation by simply holding them in your hands. You can also just stare at them, and each time your mind wanders, bring your attention back to the crystals.
9. Apply any heart chakra oils to help you stay present during your yoga, meditation, or breathwork.
10. Mindfully eat foods that will help your chakra by envisioning each one as green light going right to your heart energy center. Some great foods to use for your eating meditation include green cabbage, cucumber, green apples, asparagus, limes, chives, celery, leeks, green peppers, mint, and green salads.

Chapter 7: Healing the Throat Chakra

Correspondences

Sanskrit: Vishuddha
Meaning: Pure
Color: Blue
Seed Sound: Ham
Body Location: Throat
Element: Ether and sound
Psychological Purpose: Communication
Burden: Lies

What Does the Throat Chakra Do and Why Is It Important?

The fifth chakra in your body is the throat chakra, which affects your sense of communication. It also makes you feel comfortable speaking up for yourself. It can help you express your truth, which is one of the reasons why it's also known as the truth or vanguard chakra. The throat chakra can help teach us about honesty and integrity, which are extremely important traits to have in life.

Many people don't use these traits because they get put down by others who aren't living an honest and healthy lifestyle themselves. The throat chakra is located in the middle part of the neck. It is a very important part as it deals with your relationships with others. It's important to have this chakra open and balanced in your life to freely communicate your feelings, thoughts, and emotions without feeling threatened by anyone else around you.

Physical Effects of a Blocked Throat Chakra

When this chakra is blocked, you'll experience issues with your throat, like soreness. Sometimes you may even lose your voice. Other things you may deal with are mouth ulcers, problems with your thyroid gland, indigestion, heartburn, and even eating disorders. Hearing and dental issues aren't unheard of either. This chakra is connected to the ears, mouth, and throat, so if your Vishuddha imbalance or blockage goes unaddressed for a long while, these parts of your body will get badly affected. However, this doesn't mean you shouldn't go to a medical professional to address them, but that you should investigate doing some chakra work to help the process of healing and recovery, and more than that, help you to live and express your truth to the fullest.

Emotional Effects of a Blocked Throat Chakra

With a blocked throat chakra, you may not be able to speak your mind to others around you. You may also wind up treating other people as though they should know or understand what you're feeling and what's going on with your life, when in fact, not everyone's an actual mind reader. You may be putting too much pressure and expectation on them to understand you.

Another problem is having a hard time expressing yourself when something is bothering you. You either bottle things up or find yourself saying things that don't even make sense in the first place. You may be feeling lonely, uncomfortable with being frank with people, and even worse with yourself, and that's because you have this constant knot of fear in your stomach and threats that, more often than not, aren't real, at least not for you and your life experience. The feeling of constantly being threatened makes it easy to see how you could have shoulder and neck pain as you're constantly tense and watchful of what you say. Not only do you watch what you say, you're even mindful of what your body is saying and what your mouth isn't saying. It's a terrible way to live, and if this is you, you should definitely do something to balance this chakra so you can breathe easy. It's not worth living with constant anger at withholding your truth and paranoia.

Spiritual Effects of a Blocked Throat Chakra

Spiritually, you may feel as if you're no longer hearing from or connecting with the divine. It's an odd sensation of feeling as though all there is to you is just your physical self and nothing more. Your spirit guides may do their best to try to reach out to you, but you just can't get a single message from them, and as a result, you find yourself constantly getting into situations that could have been avoided if you could have listened to them. It's easy to argue that you don't receive messages from your spirit guides because you feel like you've never had that clairaudience ability. But the fact of the matter is, we all do. Clairaudience can manifest in a myriad of ways, and it doesn't necessarily mean that you have not experienced that before.

So, when your throat chakra is blocked, you're essentially not only cutting off yourself from putting out your truth into the world but preventing your divine spirit from reaching out to you as well. Think of your throat chakra like an ear. I know that's a little bit weird but stick with me. Your throat chakra allows you to communicate the essence of yourself to other people around you and dictate how your world will go. In other words, it is an essential energy center for manifestation. However, your throat chakra does a lot more than allow you to put out your ideas because it is a reception point for information blocks or downloads from the spirit realm that could help you achieve the things you want in life. So, when this chakra is out of balance, you may not receive clear information, and when it is completely blocked, you may feel like you're cut off from that which makes you, for we are all spirits at our very core.

What Blocks the Throat Chakra?

If you have any dirty, nasty habits like smoking and drinking, it could cause your throat chakra to close up. The meaning of the Sanskrit word for the throat chakra is purification. So, things that could block this chakra include eating unhealthy food. Also, when you think about other people in less than honorable ways, it could cause blockages in your throat chakra. So be mindful of the kind of thoughts that you entertain within yourself so that you do not generate blocks. Obviously, it is hard to tell people about the negative things that you perceive about them, and this means when push comes to shove, the temptation to lie and flatter them becomes too great. These are things that can cause an imbalance in this energy center.

What Does It Feel Like When Your Throat Chakra Is Awake and Balanced?

When you have an active throat chakra, expressing your feelings is not something you shy away from. It's not as if you do not realize there are consequences to speaking your truth, but you no longer let those things hold you back. You realize that it is not your responsibility to shield others from their emotions, and so you'll say your truth, even if they feel offended by it. This doesn't mean that you become a terrible person. It just means that you no longer allow yourself to be silenced by your fear of how others will react. If anything, balancing your throat chakra will make sure that when you communicate, you can do so not only in the fullness of truth but also with love.

Another interesting thing that happens to people who balance their throat chakra is that they start speaking loudly. When I say loud, I don't mean loud as in obnoxious, but loud as in confident. There is also a sort of musicality to the way they say things. When those who were talkative due to overactive throat chakras, when their chakra is balanced in this center, they realize they do not talk as much as they used to. They can pause and listen to what the other person has to say instead of just waiting to give their piece. Bringing balance to this energy center means you no longer indulge in gossip, and you're not the sort of person to tell unnecessary lies just to start some drama. You also stop interrupting people when they're trying to say something.

If you used to struggle with issues like voice loss, thyroid problems, neck pain, ear pain, or you had trouble with lockjaw and swallowing, you'll find that those things are now a thing of the past. All digestive issues will also cease.

Mantras and Affirmations for Unblocking the Throat Chakra

The following are affirmations that you can use to unblock your throat chakra and bring balance to it:

- I have no problems connecting with my inner knowing.
- I can speak my truth with no fear.
- I know that my voice deserves to be heard.
- I speak the truth with love.
- In everything I say, I am gentle and kind.
- I honor the fact that others have a right to express their truths.
- I honor the fact that my truth has a right to be different from others.
- I find it easy to express myself with authenticity.
- I freely allow my creativity and joy to shine through me.
- I recognize the truth whenever I encounter it.
- I speak with courage.
- My words flow gracefully.

The mantra to bring flow and balance to your throat chakra is HAM, which is the seed sound for the Vishuddha. Pronounce it H-Ah-M, not ham as in hamburger. You can also chant the sound "ee" as in "deep." Do this in the key of G for more powerful results.

Crystals and Oils

The best crystals to use to clear your throat chakra are aquamarine, turquoise, blue lace agate, blue apatite, lapis lazuli, and kyanite. The best oils to work with are Myrrh, magnolia, orange flower, lilac, sweet pea, benzoin, and frankincense.

Breathwork for the Throat Chakra

The best forms of pranayama for the throat chakra are "against the wave" breathwork or Viloma pranayama and the cooling breath. Since we've already talked about how to do the cooling breath, let's learn how to do the former.

Against the Wave Breath
1. Lie or sit in a comfortable position.
2. Split your lungs into three thirds in your mind.
3. Take a deep breath and fill only the first third of your lungs. This is the bottom-most part.
4. Hold that inhalation for three seconds. If three seconds is too long, you can hold it for two.
5. Breathe in again to fill the second part of your lungs. This is the midsection. Hold that for two seconds.
6. Take one more breath in to fill up the third part of your lungs. Make sure they are nice and full, but you do not feel any stress on them either. Hold that breath for two more seconds.
7. Empty your lungs in one long breath.
8. Take a few regular breaths so you can recover.
9. Bring your attention to your body and make sure you're feeling relaxed.
10. Again, breathe in a long breath and fill up your lungs entirely. Hold that breath for a few seconds.
11. Now empty the bottom third of your lungs. Pause for a couple of seconds.
12. Empty the middle third of your lungs and pause for a couple of seconds.
13. Exhale one more time, emptying all the air from your lungs. Pause for a couple of seconds and notice the stillness around you.

14. When your lungs tell you that they would like you to resume breathing, do so with a smooth, long inhale, and then exhale and relax.
15. Allow yourself to rest for a few moments, breathing normally before repeating the process.

Perform this exercise while you're lying on the floor in a corpse pose, also known as savasana. The corpse pose is simply lying on your back with your arms and legs outstretched, almost like a starfish.

Yoga Poses for the Throat Chakra

The best yoga poses for this chakra are:

- Baby cobra pose or Ardha bhujangasana
- Fish pose or Matsyasana
- Plow pose or Halasana

The Baby Cobra Pose

1. First, lie down on your mat on your stomach. You can rest either your forehead or your chin on the ground.
2. Put your palms on the floor, just beneath both shoulders.
3. Tighten the muscles of your core.
4. Bring your attention to your shoulder blades and bring them together.
5. Take a deep breath in as you raise your chest from your mat. Unlike the regular cobra pose, you're only going to raise your chest just enough to allow your neck and head to come off the ground so you can look in front of you.
6. Remain in that position for two breaths or more.
7. To come down, exhale as you gently bring your chest and head back to the floor or mat.

If you feel any form of strain as you perform this exercise, try keeping your feet apart even further to have less tension in your lower back.

The Fish Pose

Fish pose.
https://www.pexels.com/photo/woman-practicing-yoga-3822585/

1. Start by lying on your mat on your back.
2. Prop yourself up on your elbows. Your upper arms and the ground should be perpendicular to each other, and your palms should be on the floor.
3. Press down into the earth with your palms. If you want some more stability, you can place them beneath your butt.
4. Now drop your head backward as if you're trying to get the top of it to the floor. Your throat should be exposed and facing upward to the sky if you're doing it right.
5. Engage the muscles in your toes and legs all through this pose.
6. When you're ready to come out of it, you have to push down your four arms and lift your head away from the ground so your throat isn't exposed anymore.
7. Finally, allow your upper body to come back down to earth.

The Plow Pose

1. Lie down on your yoga mat. You may need to double it or use a blanket to make yourself more comfortable. If you opt to use a blanket, it's a good idea to have it supporting your shoulders, neck, and head.

2. Begin by placing both arms on the floor, keeping them palms down and extended toward your feet.
3. Press down into the earth with both palms, drawing on strength from your forearms to create some leverage to allow you to easily raise your legs.
4. Lift your legs to 90 degrees. Keep them there for a bit.
5. Next, raise your butt, working with your abdominal muscles to help you send your feet over your head. You want to get your feet to touch the ground at your head, if you can, and make sure your legs remain straight.
6. You can now connect your hands by interlacing the fingers while ensuring your arms don't bend. The knuckles should be drawn towards your feet while using your shoulders to strongly connect with the ground. Lengthen your pose by raising your chest a bit higher.
7. Have your shoulders gone astray? You have to bring them back into alignment one at a time by using a rocking motion, moving each one at a time. Make sure they are beneath your hips and aligned with them, and if you need to feel more stable, you can push down into your feet.
8. It is important that you DO NOT attempt to look around you from this position, or you might terribly hurt your neck, so please keep it neutral, keeping your gaze to the ceiling.
9. To come out of this pose, your arms should go back to the floor first, palms down. Then allow them to relax as you raise your feet, working with your core muscles, and then let your vertebra reconnect with the floor one at a time. Please take your time coming out of this and make sure that your feet and legs remain straight.

Chakra Meditations

For five to 15 minutes per session, you can do one or any combination of the following:

1. Chant HAM or "ee" in the key to G.

2. Choose any or several of the affirmations offered here (or create your own) and meditate on them. You can chant them or just think about what they mean to you and your life.
3. Imagine there's a brilliant blue light coming from the Vishuddha and enveloping you.
4. As you meditate, see your throat chakra as a bright blue ball. Do you notice any dark spots or areas in them? That's fine. You can simply imagine you're breathing through the chakra, taking in bright blue light and breathing out the darkness. Continue to breathe in this light until the ball is nothing but blue. You may continue breathing or stop once the ball is bright again.
5. Practice the breathwork offered here. You can do so in combination with your mantras in your mind.
6. Try meditating with the crystals mentioned before in your hands or meditating on them. You can work with just one or several. If you notice your attention has wandered from the crystal, just refocus on it, and don't beat yourself up for losing focus. It happens to even the best of us.
7. Work with the smell of the essential oils listed here. They can help with opening the chakras and helping you remain rooted in meditation.
8. Mindful eating is also an option here. Envision the meals as blue light, and as you eat, imagine all that energy going straight to work on your Vishuddha. Good blue foods are prunes, concord grapes, blueberries, blue cornmeal, and plum.

Chapter 8: Healing the Third Eye Chakra

Correspondences

Sanskrit: Ajna
Meaning: Command center
Color: Indigo
Seed Sound: Om
Body Location: Brow
Element: Light
Psychological Purpose: Intuition
Burden: Illusion

What Does the Third Eye Chakra Do and Why Is It Important?

The third eye chakra is located in the center of your forehead, situated just above the junction of your eyebrows. It is known as the seat of universal consciousness. As you might be aware, the human brain is divided into two hemispheres, the left side, and the right side. These two halves communicate with one another via a bundle of nerve fibers known as the corpus callosum. In most people, these two halves are in sync with one another and operate in tandem with one another to process sensory information from the external environment.

However, some individuals have a developing or fully developed third eye chakra which allows them to access information from outside the realm of their five senses. Since there are no physical means by which these individuals can access information (e.g., sight, sound, etc.), it may be perceived as paranormal or spiritual. It occurs when a person receives impressions of future events or places, past events, or is just exceptionally intuitive. This is extrasensory perception (ESP) which extends beyond your basic senses and allows you to receive information through other means such as telepathy (the ability to read minds) and precognition (the ability to see into the future).

The third eye acts as a doorway between our conscious and unconscious selves because it lies directly in between where the two halves of our brain communicate with one another. This doorway allows the person to consciously access information that has been stored within their unconscious self. This is the same ability that allows us to dream. This may seem a little daunting at first, but once you're familiar with the abilities of the third eye chakra, you'll be able to use this doorway to your advantage. In fact, you'll soon find yourself using this door as much as possible to manifest anything into reality.

The third eye chakra also plays a central role in mediating trance states, a state between being awake and asleep. This is an important trait of the third eye chakra because it allows the individual to utilize a form of heightened consciousness that is often linked up with being hypnotic. This ability adds to the third eye's role as a doorway between the conscious and unconscious mind, allowing us to easily enter the trance state.

We're all familiar with what happens when our body enters hypnosis: we begin to lose all ability for rational thought and start recalling past events, visions, or even conversations that we've had with other people. Trance states are also utilized in magick by some individuals who use them in their rituals or spells. It's also used in hypnotherapy, where a hypnotist assists a client in entering a trance state to help them overcome an issue. In all this, the third eye chakra is key in helping the individual to achieve these trance states.

The third eye chakra is also associated with higher consciousness and self-awareness, which is why it's linked to your ability to see clairvoyantly and your intuition. This association can also be tied to having a photographic memory and exceptional recall ability, which are linked to more advanced states of being with your third eye chakra.

This chakra works in conjunction with the pineal gland found in the center of your brain, just above your third eye. The pineal gland has many roles within the human body, but one very important function is releasing melatonin at night. The melatonin released by the pineal gland allows us to enter sleep states more easily and effectively. This helps us heal our bodies and recuperate from physical injury and mental strain so we can have more energy for the day.

Physical Effects of a Blocked Third Eye Chakra

A blocked third eye chakra will affect your entire body because it is such a central component of your being. This is especially true for individuals who regularly work with the third eye chakra because they rely on their ability to access information through other means to perform their jobs or tasks (e.g., meditation, yoga, etc.).

The physical effects of a blocked third eye chakra are easy to spot: headaches, fatigue, dizziness, and nausea may plague the individual for no apparent reason whatsoever.

Excessive sleepiness or insomnia are also signs of a blocked third eye chakra. Sleepiness is likely the result of lack of sleep, but insomnia can be a sign of nightmare presence or issues with dreaming, which points to third eye issues.

There are also physical effects that may occur in people who have reached the level of spiritual enlightenment. When the pineal gland releases enough melatonin, it can affect your body in difficult and uncomfortable ways: it causes you to experience changes in your vision and other sensory experiences. You also feel as though some part of you has been pulled out or removed from your physical body, which can lead to feelings of suffocation or dread. This can be a very uncomfortable experience for some people, and many never get over this feeling.

Other issues include hallucination, overthinking, a sense of being lost, constant self-doubt, paranoia, constant tension in the brow area, hearing issues, sinus issues, eye issues, headaches and migraine, trouble focusing and sleeping, issues with thinking through things, confusion, and so on. Please be sure to check in with your medical doctor before deciding your issues are purely the sort that can be fixed only with third eye meditations.

Emotional Effects of a Blocked Third Eye Chakra

The emotional effect of a blocked third eye chakra can be just as difficult to deal with as the physical symptoms. Emotions can change dramatically for the individual experiencing a blocked third eye chakra, and these emotions can even result in mood disorders. If you find that your emotions change rapidly and you're having difficulty controlling them, this may indicate that your third eye chakra is blocked. It is especially true if you've had problems dealing with stress or anxiety in the past.

A blocked ajna also affects your ability to think clearly, which means that you may start to experience memory loss. If you experience this, you'll likely have some very difficult days, as you may find that you're unable to recall information that is important to your life or has happened in the past.

Individuals who have poor emotional regulation are likely to find themselves in an endless cycle of "going up" or "coming down." These extreme highs and lows can be hard to break out of because they can lead to severe depression or anxiety, which are difficult conditions to overcome.

Believers in the metaphysical have noticed that a blocked third eye chakra can increase the belief that one's life is predestined and a lack of faith in their ability to change anything in their life. This can be a particularly difficult emotional state for those who have reached higher levels of spiritual enlightenment because they may experience the belief that they cannot influence their lives or experiences.

In some cases, people who have a blocked third eye chakra may even go as far as to experience some form of psychosis. This is common amongst those who harbor a belief that they are being led by an unseen influence around them and those who have had a particularly traumatic life event that has affected their perception of reality.

Spiritual Effects of a Blocked Third Eye Chakra

The most spiritual manifestation of a blocked third eye chakra is a feeling of being disconnected from the universe. At this point, you'll find that you have a hard time connecting with others and the world around you; you may even seem to be alone on planet Earth. This can easily happen when your third eye chakra is blocked because your connection with spirit has been disrupted.

Some people who identify as New Agers or Wiccans also see their faith as being threatened by an inner blockage of their third eye chakra. This can cause them to question what they believe in more than ever before and make them look for other explanations for certain events that have occurred in their lives.

Another spiritual manifestation of a blocked third eye chakra is difficulty in connecting with your spirit guides or your higher self. If you're having trouble doing this, you'll know that there's a problem with your third eye chakra. Contacting or creating a relationship with your spirit guide or higher self is extremely important because they can give you the assistance you need to effectively heal the third eye chakra.

When the third eye chakra is blocked, individuals may also feel as though they're living on another plane of existence. Their perspective of their surroundings and what goes on around them changes dramatically and can even lead to feelings of paranoia and fear. People who suffer from this may start to feel as though they're being watched or that someone or something is attempting to harm them.

If your third eye chakra is blocked and you have a strong spiritual connection with your higher self, this can be extremely difficult for you. You may find that you're unable to access any great wisdom or use the power of your mind in any way. For example, if you have an idea or creative inspiration, you might be unable to do anything with it, which can be frustrating and lead to feelings of disappointment in your life. This is especially true for those who have reached a higher level of spiritual enlightenment. If you believe that you're at the highest level of spiritual awareness, you may find that a blocked third eye chakra can create feelings of inferiority, depression, and hopelessness.

What Does It Feel Like When Your Third Eye Chakra Is Awake and Balanced?

When your third eye chakra is balanced, you'll likely have "supernatural" experiences that feel strikingly real. You may start to experience a spiritual awakening and be able to hear sounds from the universe and see things that are invisible to others around you. You'll naturally have a very high level of intuition when your third eye chakra is balanced, and you may even begin to experience vivid dreams.

It's worth taking the time to work on this energy center because when you do, and it's working as it should, you'll feel as though you're on a spiritual high. You're more in tune with your surroundings, including the people and creatures around you, and you feel at peace with everything in your life. If you've ever had a problem in your life, you can use this heightened spiritual awareness to focus on those problems and begin working to solve them. You'll immediately see the results of your actions, which will encourage you to keep going until you've resolved all the issues that have held back growth in your life.

As you continue to open up your third eye chakra, you might find it easier for you to meditate. In fact, those who have a clear third eye chakra can enter a meditative state very quickly, during which they can focus on the things that are important to them. With this level of focus, it's easier for these individuals to take action and make changes in their lives as needed. When things are balanced with your Ajna, you're more likely to be able to handle any emotional issues or problems that may come along during your life because you'll be able to always remain centered and in control of your emotions.

Mantras and Affirmations for Unblocking the Third Eye Chakra

The following are affirmations you can use to help open up this center and keep it in balance:

- I am balanced from all directions – north, east, south, and west.
- I am relaxed and serene, living my life without worry or care.
- My third eye chakra is open and working properly.
- I trust my intuition as I make decisions in all areas of my life. My mind and body work synergistically with my spirit.
- I am surrounded by positive energy as I go through each day.
- My third eye chakra is open and allows me to fully experience my life at its fullest potential.
- I am aware of all that exists around me, and I'm able to take advantage of it. I am prepared for anything and everything that comes my way.
- I know the presence of an unseen world, but it does not prevent me from living in this one.
- I use the energy of spirit to make better decisions in all areas of my life.
- My third eye chakra is awake and working properly.
- Miracles are present in my life, always.

As for great mantras, you can chant the seed sound of this chakra, which is OM (pronounced Oh-M), or you can just go "mmmmm" over and over, in your mind or out loud. Do this in the key of A for good results.

Crystals and Oils

The best crystals to work on this chakra with are clear quartz, amethyst, sodalite, black obsidian, labradorite, lepidolite, and iolite.

As for oils, work with juniper, elemi, frankincense, bay laurel, marjoram, lavender, patchouli, cedarwood, and clary sage.

Breathwork for the Third Eye Chakra

The best forms of pranayama for this center are Nadi shodhana or alternate nostril breathing, which we've already described, and Bhastrika pranayama. Bhastrika means "bellows."

Bellows Breathwork

Before we begin, it's important to do this one on an empty stomach and after you've had a bowel movement. This is the optimal condition to be in if you want great results.

1. You ought to perform this exercise while sitting on a comfortable chair. You should make sure that your body is sitting right above your waistline and your spine remains nice and long-reaching for the ceiling. Gently close your eyes.
2. As forcefully as you can, breathe in and out through your nose while making sure you're not straining in any way.
3. Continue breathing in and out this way, calling on the muscles of your diaphragm. Your stomach should rise with each inhalation as your diaphragm comes down, and then it should collapse as the diaphragm goes up. You should try to make these movements more dramatic than usual. If you're doing it right, your nose should be making a fair bit of noise. Make sure to keep the rhythm of your breathing even, and you should be in control of the whole process.
4. Continue breathing this way for a total of ten inhales and exhales. That makes up an entire round of this breathwork.
5. Spend a few moments breathing normally, and then get back to another round.

Yoga Poses for the Third Eye Chakra

The best poses for your third eye chakra include:

- The child's pose or balasana
- The puppy pose or Uttana shishosana

- The "legs up the wall" pose or Viparita Karani

The Child's Pose

- Sit with both shins tucked beneath you on your yoga mat. Make sure to keep both knees wide at the edges of your mat.
- Gently move both hands in the front, but make sure that you're still sitting on your heels as you do this.
- When you find you can't move any further, allow your upper body, head, and arms to collapse into the earth as you splay your fingers and press them into the floor as well.
- With each breath in, imagine your spine growing longer. Imagine your head is reaching for the front of the room and your tailbone reaching for the rear, so your torso stretches properly.
- With each breath out, feel even more rooted in the earth.
- Continue this way for the next three to five breaths (or more if you feel up to it) until you're totally relaxed and grounded in the here and now.

The Puppy Pose

1. Start with your hands and knees on your mat. Remember, your hips and knees should be in alignment with each other.
2. Walk forward with just your hands, keeping your hips in place. Keep going until your chest or forehead come as close to the ground as you can manage, even better if they can touch the earth. If you're flexible, try to rest your chin on the earth.
3. Spread your hops apart gently and take three to five deep breaths.

The Legs Up the Wall Pose

1. Begin by lying down on your back. You should be close to a wall, with your rear touching it, or close enough to it so you can keep a long spine through this pose.

2. Your legs should be stretched up against the wall, with both feet flexed skywards.
3. You can let your arms just hang by your sides on the floor, or you can move them higher to be in line with both shoulders.
4. Remain in this pose for as long as it feels comfortable.

Third Eye Chakra Meditations

Remember, you need at least five minutes and at most 15 minutes for each of these exercises; you can also mix7 and match as needed for more interesting and exploding results with this chakra.

1. Chant "OM" while you're seated in lotus, or repeat it over and over in your mind.
2. Choose any or some of the affirmations in this chapter to contemplate or chant. Feel free to craft some of your own if you'd prefer.
3. Envision a bright indigo light that shines from your third eye, enveloping you from head to toe in its brilliance, infusing you with its energy, and making you more receptive to all things spiritual and good.
4. Meditate and envision a bright indigo ball that sits in the middle of your brow, glowing powerfully. If you notice any black spots in it, breathe them out with each exhale, and breathe in more powerful indigo light with each inhale until the orb shines with no blemish or spots anymore. For better results, imagine that while you may be using your nose to breathe, you're breathing light through your third eye.
5. Use the recommended breathwork in this chapter.
6. Meditate with the crystals or meditate on them.
7. Amplify your meditations by working with the recommended essential oils.
8. Practice mindful eating, envisioning the food as indigo light going into you. See its energy move up into your third eye, strengthening it, balancing it, and removing all blocks. Here are the foods that are good to eat for this purpose:

all-natural blue foods, purple kale, purple carrots, purple cabbage, purple grapes, and eggplant.

Chapter 9: Healing the Crown Chakra

Correspondences

Sanskrit: Sahasrara
Meaning: Thousandfold
Color: White or Violet
Seed Sound: None
Body Location: Top of your head
Element: Thought
Psychological Purpose: Understanding
Burden: Attachment

What Does the Crown Chakra Do and Why Is It Important?

The seventh chakra is located at the top of your head and governs spirituality, truthfulness in communication, and coordination with the higher self. It also deals with intuition, wisdom, and understanding of how your life fits into a larger pattern or purpose. Those who have healthy crown chakras can make difficult decisions with grace and precision because they are not attached to material things or outcomes. They are interested in what they know regardless of external factors like money or status.

This energy center is associated with detachment and transcendence. It is crucial in meditation. Think of it as being an anchor to your spiritual energy, which connects us to the Divine. In Eastern philosophy, particularly in Buddhism, it's thought that when we detach from worldly attachments, we can directly experience God's love for us. If you're having trouble staying grounded or feeling detached from everyday life (or even if you just want to try something new), meditating on the crown chakra can help reorient yourself back into physical reality while keeping you in touch with the spiritual reality.

The crown chakra is the crown jewel of your energy system, and when it is functioning at optimal levels, you'll have an easier time connecting with your spiritual self while meditating or practicing yoga, or simply navigating through life. It's also likely that you'll be more sensitive to what others are thinking and feeling, and other people may feel as though you always have an answer for everything. That's because you're connected to the realm of spirit, which is where every other thing in life flows from. Spirit is all here and now and never "there" or "then"; therefore, you'll have access to actual eternal truths and the truth that lies within one and all. You'll also understand your true motivations and will no longer indulge in activities that take you away from your highest good. You'll no longer waste your energy on meaningless things when you're using your crown chakra energy properly.

For instance, someone may want to spend more time with their family but believe that before they can do that, they need to make sure that they make more than enough money to take care of them. When their crown chakra works as it should, they come to realize that the way to spend time with family is to manage their time accordingly – and not waste it by always being buried in work.

Or you may think you need to hop from your old relationship right into another one, but with a working crown chakra, you come to realize that the love you seek is within you and that you can give it to yourself right away instead of waiting for the "right" person to come along and assign them a responsibility that is actually yours. Let's sum it up this way: When your crown chakra is working as it should, you're "woke" to all the BS, and that includes your own.

Physical Effects of a Blocked Crown Chakra

When you have a blocked crown chakra, you may experience frequent headaches, migraines, difficulty focusing, dizziness, lightheadedness or vertigo, problems in thinking clearly or making decisions, and increased sensitivity to light or sound (which may lead to irritability, anger, depression, and restlessness), and an increased risk of viral infections (colds, flu, etc.) as your immune system is compromised. Those who don't address the blocks and imbalances in the crown chakra can wind up contracting illnesses that may seem more difficult than usual to recover from. If this happens, it's important to dig a little deeper into why your crown chakra is blocked and work on resolving those issues to move forward toward better health.

You could also have trouble with unhealthy attachments and may be prone to addictions. Unfortunately, this may mean that you're addicted to unhealthy food or other things as well, such as drugs and alcohol.

Emotional Effects of a Blocked Crown Chakra

If your crown chakra is blocked, you may begin to feel emotionally unstable and frustrated with people who don't seem to have the same goals in mind as you. You'll often be pulled into all kinds of energy-draining situations because it feels safe and familiar. Unfortunately, this kind of situation leads you straight away from your ideal life path.

A blocked crown chakra also means that there is a lack of knowledge about what really matters in life and how to live harmoniously with others. At this point, you may feel alone and even alienated from others, and that goes for close friends, family, and complete strangers.

The root of these feelings is a lack of self-confidence, which leads to low self-esteem. Not only that, but with a blocked crown chakra, you'll often be unsure about where you stand in your relationships, both romantic and friendly, because you have no clear sense of what is important to you.

Spiritual Effects of a Blocked Crown Chakra

You'll notice that you have difficulty connecting with your inner self-knowing and your guides. You'll also find that you're plagued by nightmares that can feel all too real, or on the flip side, you can barely remember your dreams. If you think remembering your dreams isn't important, think again. Dreams often come with very important messages we need to help us in life; they may also present clues to problems we may be dealing with that we can't fix with our logical, rational minds. So, when you can't remember your dreams, you'll see how this would spill over and affect everything that you do in the physical world.

What Does It Feel Like When Your Crown Chakra Is Awake and Balanced?

Your energy is directed upward and outward when you have a healthy crown chakra. You're grounded in the present moment and can see the big picture of what's happening around you. You can easily detach from any situation that is no longer serving you to live your life with purpose.

You feel more connected to your higher power and are more apt to enjoy meditation, yoga, or other spiritual practices. You're likely to be more intuitive, your instincts are right on target, and you've got wisdom that comes from understanding your surroundings. Your intuition will guide you toward making good decisions while being able to keep yourself free from emotional attachments.

Spiritual Awakening is more than just a buzzword. It's a journey that you take with the intention of finding peace and contentment in the present moment, and your crown chakra is the key. When you're awake to the crown chakra, you'll be able to focus on what matters most, not what matters right now. Because what matters right now is often fleeting, your highest wisdom will tell you to find a way to detach yourself from it so that it doesn't become who you're.

You're going to come across some situations in life that are not quite as they seem, and you'll also come across people who are not quite as they seem. It's difficult to keep your mind from being completely taken over by these things, but there is a way to bring your crown chakra in balance simply by reminding yourself that you know exactly what's real and what isn't.

When you let go of the idea that what you're experiencing is something that "is" real, it will help you detach from your thoughts completely so that you can live in the present moment with no past or future and no expectations of "right" or "wrong" outcome. You may not "get" everything about every situation in life, but you'll be able to observe it without judgment or expectations.

Mantras and Affirmations for Unblocking the Crown Chakra

The following are affirmations you can use when you're working on your crown chakra:

- I have all the answers.
- My instincts are right on, and I know what's best for me.
- I am free to be and do exactly what I want, with no strings attached.
- My crown chakra is open, and my connection to my spirit guides is strong.
- My intuition guides me through life, and I don't need anyone else's influence to get me there.
- I don't want it anymore if it isn't healthy for me.
- Yesterday isn't any more real than tomorrow, so I let things just be as they are.
- It doesn't matter how things turn out. Everything will be alright.
- I'm so happy about things being this way.
- I know that I am worthy of love and acceptance as I am.
- I am not seeking for anyone to give me meaning or purpose because I already know that none of these things are mine.
- Every drop of divinity is within me.

- I am connected to my source.
- I give out love and light in every aspect of my life.

The mantra you should work with is the sound "NG," as in sing. Chant that in the key of B to activate and balance the Sahasrara.

Crystals and Oils

You can use fluorite, charoite, white calcite, white agate, clear quartz, lapis lazuli, amethyst, lepidolite, selenite, sugilite, labradorite, and moonstone. The best essential oils are elemi, benzoin, anise seed, basil, spikenard, palo santo, sandalwood, frankincense, myrtle, and galbanum.

Breathwork for the Crown Chakra

The best breathwork to do for your crown chakra includes:

- Sitali pranayama, or the cooling breath
- Sitkari pranayama, or the sipping breath

You can refer to the instructions already given on how to perform the cooling breath.

The Sipping Breath

- Sit on a chair or in the lotus position in a quiet place wearing comfortable clothes. Gently close your eyes.
- Take some deep breaths so you can relax your body and mind. Take your time with this, and only move on when you're nice and grounded.
- Part your lips slightly, and let your tongue peek out of your mouth by three-quarters of an inch.
- Breathe in through your mouth. The air should flow past your tongue, whipping around your teeth. You'll notice a sound like sipping or hissing if you're doing it right. There's no need to force the sound; just relax into it.
- Close your lips and gulp down the air when you're done breathing in.
- Hold your breath for two to three seconds, keeping your tongue against the softer palate in your mouth.

- Now it's time to breathe out. Do this through your nose and make sure you completely empty your lungs while your lips stay sealed. This is a full round of the sipping breath. You can do a few more rounds and take breaks as needed.

Ideally, when you're first starting, your inhale and exhale should last about the same time. As you get better at this, your exhale should last twice as long as the inhale. You only need about eight to ten rounds to begin repeating the benefits of the cooling breath. It's a good idea to do about 15 to 20 rounds when you're more proficient, once when you wake up and once before you go to bed.

Yoga Poses for the Crown Chakra

Some of the best poses to help you open and balance your crown chakra include:

- Sasangasana or the rabbit stand pose
- Makarasana or crocodile pose
- Gomukhasana or cow face pose

The Rabbit Stand Pose

1. Get down on your knees on your yoga mat. Keep your knees together.
2. Bring the top of your head down to touch the ground.
3. Reach backward and grab your heels with your hands.
4. Remain in this position for as long as it feels comfortable.
5. When you're ready to come out, release your heels and slowly raise your head from the floor.

The Crocodile Pose

1. Start by sitting on your shins on your mat, with your knees together.
2. Stretch out your hands to touch the floor in front of you.
3. Now, you need to stretch your legs out behind you, staying on the balls of your feet.
4. Bring your legs down to the ground and flex your feet to keep their tops on the mat.

5. Now allow your hips to drop to the floor, followed by your belly, chest, and shoulders. Make sure you're looking down at the ground, and both elbows are by your sides. Your palms should be in contact with the floor.
6. Now, move both hands to your front and slowly cross them over each other. Rest your head on your crossed arms. Remember, you should still be face down.
7. If you prefer, you can let your arms be by your sides while you push your forehead into your mat and stretch out both legs for a longer back.
8. When you're ready, come out of this pose slowly.

The Cow Face Pose

Cow face pose.
Kennguru, CC BY 3.0 https://creativecommons.org/licenses/by/3.0 via Wikimedia Commons: https://commons.wikimedia.org/wiki/File:Gomukhasana_Yoga-Asana_Nina-Mel.jpg

1. Begin in the lotus position. You want your right leg to be over the left one.
2. Next, slide both knees so that they are in alignment with your midline. If you need some help doing this, you could scooch forward a bit on both hands and knees.

3. Lift your right arm, raising it to the sky.
4. Bend your right elbow as you move your right hand behind the neck. Working with your left hand, you can nudge your elbow a bit, so it lines up with your center, just like your knees.
5. Raise your left arm out to the left, bending it at the elbow, and then move the left arm up to the middle of your back.
6. If you can swing it, clasp your hands behind you.
7. Pull your elbows to the middle and do your best not to let your head push forward. You can avoid this by using your right hand as support for the back of your head. Don't struggle with this, and make sure that you keep your breath even.
8. When you're ready, relax both arms on an in-breath, and then do the pose again, switching sides.

Crown Chakra Meditations

Do the following for five to 15 minutes. Remember you can pick one or combine them as convenient for you.

1. Chant "NG" in meditation or make the sound in your mind.
2. Meditate on the affirmations provided here or the ones you come up with. You can say them aloud or just think of what they mean to you.
3. Imagine a white or violet light coming out of the top of your head, wrapping your whole body with its light, and supercharging your body.
4. As you practice breathing meditation, envision your crown chakra as a white or violet ball of light. Notice if there are any dark areas in there. Take a deep breath in and imagine you're breathing in white or violet light through that chakra. As you breathe out, imagine you're breathing out all that darkness. Continue this way until time's up or you have exhaled all the darkness out of you
5. Use the breathwork outline in this chapter.

6. Practice the yoga poses while contemplating the mantra and/or visualizing the white or violet light.
7. Meditate with crystals or on them.
8. Amplify all your meditations by using an essential oil or meditate on the scents of the oil.
9. Practice mindful eating and see the food as white or violet light going into you as you eat, moving up to your crown chakra to make it function optimally. Here are foods to eat: beet tops, garlic, purple grapes, plums, broccoli, blackberry, coconut, mushrooms, onions, ginger, and lychee.

Chapter 10: Your Chakra Balancing Routine

So, you've gotten a lot of information and action points, and you may be feeling a bit overwhelmed about what to do first or where to go from here. Don't worry because you're about to get a lovely 7-day daily routine to help you with each of your chakras. No, this isn't going to be a one-chakra-a-day thing. You need to spend time with each chakra before you move on to the next. So, we're going to spend a week on each chakra. If you insist on working more than once a week, you can just pick what works for you, but note that you should take your time with this. So, let's begin.

Root Chakra Routine

Day 1

1. Chant LAM for five minutes for at least 15 minutes tops in the morning.
2. Put a drop of rose essential oil on your collar or on the back of your ears after your shower.
3. Do some root chakra breathing for just five minutes at noon, envisioning red light all around you.
4. Meditate for five minutes with a ruby or some other root chakra crystal in hand while contemplating any of the affirmations mentioned.

5. At the end of the day, chant "Oh" for five to 15 minutes.

Day 2

1. Chant "Oh" first thing in the morning for five to 15 minutes.
2. For five minutes, visualize your root chakra and do the chakra color breathing to get rid of any blockage you see in your mind's eye.
3. Pick one affirmation to contemplate for five minutes.
4. Eat something red today, meditating on each bite as it goes down.
5. At the end of the day, chant LAM.

Day 3

1. Start your day by contemplating one of the affirmations given in this book. Take at least five minutes, at most 15 minutes.
2. Go outside barefoot and stand on the natural earth for ten minutes, soaking in the earth's energy.
3. Do the cooling breath while repeating the LAM mantra in your mind.
4. Do the garland pose for just five minutes.
5. Wrap up your day by contemplating a different affirmation.

Day 4

1. Chant LAM at the start of your day for ten minutes.
2. Practice mindful eating with one of the red chakra foods.
3. Do the standing forward bend pose for five minutes.
4. Sit for 15 minutes, envisioning yourself being enveloped by bright, beautiful red light.
5. End your day by repeating a mantra out loud to yourself while you fall asleep.

Day 5

1. Chant LAM for 15 minutes to start your day.
2. Read all the affirmations for the root chakra over and over for five minutes. Feel the words you say.

3. Work with some essential oil and sit and meditate on the smell and the way it makes you feel in the root chakra area.
4. Do the garland pose while mentally chanting LAM for five minutes.
5. Wrap up your day by chanting "Oh," as you fall asleep.

Day 6

1. Start by chanting LAM for five minutes, then "Oh" for five, and wrap up with LAM again for five minutes, for a total of 15 minutes.
2. Go walk around barefoot outside, and with each step, envision red light coming out of the earth, moving up your legs and right into your root chakra.
3. Eat a root chakra meal mindfully.
4. Do the standing forward bend pose for just five minutes.
5. Go to bed chanting LAM, then "Oh," then LAM, for five minutes each.

Day 7

1. Start your day breathing in red light into your root chakra for 15 minutes while mentally focusing on the mantra LAM.
2. Head outside and lie down on your back on the grass. Soak up the earth's energy.
3. Do both the garland and standing forward bend poses, cycling back and forth for ten minutes.
4. Do the alternate breath technique for ten minutes today.
5. Go to bed chanting "Oh," as you fall asleep.

Sacral Chakra Routine

Day 1

1. Chant VAM for five minutes.
2. Do the skull shining breath while envisioning yourself surrounded by orange light.
3. Meditate with a sacral chakra crystal for five minutes.

4. Do the victorious breath for five minutes while working with essential oil.

5. Chant "OO" at the end of your day for five minutes.

Day 2

1. Chant "OO" for five minutes.

2. Perform the victorious breath while doing the chakra clearing meditation.

3. Meditate on the scent of a sacral chakra essential oil and feel how it affects your sacral chakra. Do this for five minutes.

4. Do the skull shining breath for five minutes.

5. Wrap up your day by chanting **VAM** for five minutes before bed.

Day 3

1. Contemplate one of the affirmations for five minutes.

2. Do the bound angle pose for five minutes.

3. Work with crystal and essential oils in a five-minute meditation.

4. Meditate and visualize your sacral chakra clearing up and becoming active and clear.

5. Chant **VAM** for five minutes before bed. Do nothing else after. Just go to sleep.

Day 4

1. Mentally chant **VAM** as you do a breathing meditation for ten minutes

2. Do the dancing goddess pose for five minutes.

3. Practice meditative eating with some or any of the sacral chakra foods.

4. For five minutes, supercharge yourself with some orange light.

5. Wrap up your day by contemplating an affirmation that calls to you the most.

Day 5

1. Mentally chant "OO" as you do a breathing meditation for ten minutes
2. Do the bound angle and dancing goddess poses for five minutes each.
3. Choose one affirmation to focus on from this book and contemplate it for ten minutes.
4. Meditate on a sacral crystal for ten minutes.
5. Wrap up your day by contemplating two affirmations that mean a lot to you.

Day 6

1. Pick one mantra and meditate on it for five minutes.
2. Breathe in orange light for 15 minutes.
3. Put some water in a bowl and contemplate it for five minutes. You can also touch it if you want.
4. Sit with a crystal and envision its energy as orange light, enveloping you for five minutes.
5. Chant the VAM mantra for 15 minutes, allowing it to take over you.

Day 7

1. Chant VAM for five minutes, "OO" for five minutes, and VAM for five more minutes.
2. Alternate between the dancing goddess and bound angle poses for 15 minutes.
3. Contemplate whatever it is you desire the most in the world right now as you repeat to yourself, "I deserve all the good I desire."
4. Perform the skull shining breath for five minutes while wearing a crystal and essential oil.
5. Wrap up your day by mentally chanting VAM, then "OO," and VAM once more for five minutes each.

Solar Plexus Routine

Day 1

1. Chant RAM for five minutes first thing in the morning.
2. Apply some essential oil for this chakra to your collar, and then do the bumblebee breath for five minutes.
3. Do the chakra clearing exercise where you get rid of all darkness or blocks in your solar plexus chakra.
4. Contemplate an affirmation and what it means to you for five minutes.
5. Wrap up your day with a five-minute chant of "AH."

Day 2

1. Chant "AH" for five minutes when you get up.
2. Perform the alternate leg raise pose, taking breaks as often as needed. Do this for five minutes.
3. Repeat all the affirmations to yourself for five minutes, dwelling on what they mean to you.
4. Pick an essential oil and meditate on it for five minutes.
5. End the day by mentally chanting RAM.

Day 3

1. Pick one affirmation to contemplate for five minutes upon waking up.
2. Practice meditative eating using one of the solar plexus chakra foods.
3. Pick a crystal and meditate on it for ten minutes, soaking in its energy.
4. Surround yourself with brilliant yellow light to charge your chakra for five minutes.
5. End the day focusing on a different affirmation than you began with for five minutes before bed.

Day 4

1. Mentally chant "AH" for ten minutes in the morning.
2. Do the cobra pose for five minutes while imagining yellow light surrounding you.

3. Choose one affirmation and focus on it while you walk outside for ten minutes.

4. Pick a new crystal if you've got one and contemplate it for five minutes.

5. End your day by mentally chanting **RAM** for ten minutes.

Day 5

1. In your mind, chant **RAM** in the morning for five minutes.

2. Do the alternate leg raise pose for five minutes while mentally focusing on the seed sound **RAM**.

3. Work with both essential oil and a crystal of your choice, meditating on them and connecting with your solar plexus chakra for ten minutes.

4. Do the cobra pose for five minutes while you meditate on the sound "AH."

5. End your day chanting "AH" in your mind for five minutes before bed.

Day 6

1. Chant **RAM** for ten minutes and feel how your solar plexus reacts.

2. Pick two affirmations that resonate with you and contemplate them for ten minutes each while breathing in yellow light.

3. Practice meditative eating with one or some of the solar plexus foods.

4. Engage your solar plexus with your sense of smell by meditating on an essential oil's scent for five minutes.

5. Wrap up your day by chanting "AH" for ten minutes and feel how that affects you.

Day 7

1. Start your day chanting **RAM**, then "AH," then **RAM** again for five minutes each.

2. Alternate between the cobra pose and alternate leg raise for 15 minutes.

3. Do the chakra clearing visualization for five minutes today.

4. Do some meditative eating with the right yellow foods.

5. End your day chanting "AH," then RAM, then "AH" for five minutes each.

Heart Chakra Routine

Day 1
1. Chant **YAM** for five minutes first thing in the morning.
2. Apply some essential oil to your collar, and then do the three-part breath for five minutes.
3. Do the chakra clearing exercise where you get rid of all darkness or blocks in your heart chakra.
4. Contemplate an affirmation and what it means to you for five minutes.
5. Wrap up your day with a five-minute chant of "AY."

Day 2
1. Chant "AY" for five minutes when you wake up.
2. Perform the camel pose for five minutes, taking breaks as often as needed.
3. Repeat all the affirmations to yourself for five minutes, dwelling on what they mean to you.
4. Pick an essential oil and meditate on it for five minutes.
5. End the day by mentally chanting **YAM**.

Day 3
1. Pick one affirmation to contemplate for five minutes upon waking up.
2. Practice meditative eating using one of the heart chakra foods.
3. Pick a crystal and meditate on it for ten minutes, soaking in its energy.
4. Do the cat/cow pose for five minutes.
5. End the day focusing on a different affirmation than you began with for five minutes before bed.

Day 4
1. Mentally chant "AY" for ten minutes in the morning.

2. Do the bridge pose for five minutes while imagining green light surrounding you.

3. Choose one affirmation and focus on it while you walk outside for ten minutes.

4. Pick a new crystal if you've got one and contemplate it for five minutes.

5. End your day by mentally chanting **YAM** for ten minutes.

Day 5

1. In your mind, chant **YAM** in the morning for five minutes.

2. Do the bridge pose for five minutes while mentally focusing on the seed sound **YAM**.

3. Work with both essential oil and a crystal of your choice, meditating on them and connecting with your heart chakra as you do so for ten minutes.

4. Do the cat/cow pose for five minutes while you meditate on the sound "AY."

5. End your day chanting "AY" in your mind for five minutes before bed.

Day 6

1. Chant **YAM** for ten minutes and feel how your heart chakra reacts.

2. Pick two affirmations that resonate with you and contemplate them for ten minutes each while breathing in green light.

3. Practice meditative eating with one or some of the heart chakra foods.

4. Engage your heart energy center with your sense of smell by meditating on an essential oil's scent for five minutes.

5. Wrap up your day by chanting "AY" for ten minutes and feel how that affects you.

Day 7

1. Start your day by chanting **YAM**, then "AY," then **YAM** again for five minutes each.

2. Alternate between the cat/cow, camel, and bridge poses for 15 minutes.

3. Do the chakra clearing visualization for five minutes today.
4. Do some meditative eating with the right green foods.
5. End your day chanting "AY," then YAM, then "AY" for five minutes each.

Throat Chakra Routine

Day 1

1. In the morning, chant HAM for five minutes at least, 15 minutes tops.
2. Put a drop of essential oil on your collar or at the back of your ears after your shower.
3. Do some throat chakra breathing for just five minutes at noon, envisioning blue light all around you.
4. Meditate for five minutes with a throat chakra crystal in hand while contemplating any of the affirmations.
5. At the end of the day, chant "EE" for five to 15 minutes.

Day 2

1. Chant "EE" first thing in the morning – for five to 15 minutes.
2. For five minutes, visualize your throat chakra and do the chakra color breathing to get rid of any blockage you see in your mind's eye.
3. Pick one affirmation to contemplate for five minutes.
4. Eat something blue today, meditating on each bite as it goes down.
5. At the end of the day, chant HAM.

Day 3

1. Start your day by contemplating one of the affirmations given in this book. Take at least five minutes, at most 15 minutes.
2. Envelope yourself in blue light to charge your chakra for five minutes.
3. Do the against-the-wave breath while repeating the HAM mantra in your mind.

4. Do the baby cobra pose for just five minutes.

5. Wrap up your day by contemplating a different affirmation for five minutes.

Day 4

1. Chant HAM at the start of your day for ten minutes.

2. Practice mindful eating with one of the blue chakra foods.

3. Do the fish pose for five minutes.

4. Sit for 15 minutes, envisioning yourself being enveloped by bright, beautiful blue light.

5. End your day by repeating a mantra out loud to yourself before sleeping.

Day 5

1. Chant HAM for 15 minutes to start your day.

2. Read all the affirmations for the throat chakra over and over for five minutes. Feel the words you say.

3. Work with some essential oil and sit and meditate on the smell and the way it makes you feel in the throat chakra area.

4. Do the plow pose while mentally chanting HAM for five minutes.

5. Wrap up your day by chanting "EE" as you fall asleep.

Day 6

1. Start by chanting HAM for five minutes, then "EE" for five, and wrap up with HAM again for five minutes, for a total of 15 minutes.

2. Go barefoot for a walk outside, and with each step, envision blue light coming down from the sky, moving down through the top of your head, and coming to rest in your throat chakra.

3. Eat a throat chakra meal mindfully.

4. Do the fish and baby cobra poses for just five minutes, alternating between the two.

5. Go to bed chanting HAM, then "EE," then HAM, for five minutes each.

Day 7

1. Start your day by breathing in blue light into your root chakra for 15 minutes while mentally focusing on the mantra HAM.
2. Head outside and lie down on your back on the grass. Soak up the sky's energy.
3. Do the fish, plow, and baby cobra poses, cycling back and forth for 15 minutes.
4. Do the against-the-wave breath technique for ten minutes today.
5. Go to bed chanting "EE" as you fall asleep.

Third Eye Chakra Routine

Day 1

1. Chant OM for five minutes.
2. Do the bellows breath while envisioning yourself surrounded by indigo light.
3. Meditate with a third eye chakra crystal for five minutes.
4. Breathe in indigo light for five minutes while working with essential oil.
5. Chant "MMMM" at the end of your day for five minutes.

Day 2

1. Chant "MMMM" for five minutes.
2. Perform the bellows breath while doing the chakra clearing meditation.
3. Meditate on the scent of a third eye chakra essential oil for five minutes and feel how it affects you.
4. Do the child's pose for five minutes.
5. Wrap up your day by chanting "OM" for five minutes before bed.

Day 3

1. Contemplate one of the affirmations for five minutes.
2. Do the puppy pose for five minutes.
3. Work with a crystal and essential oils in a five-minute

meditation.

4. Meditate and visualize your chakra clearing up and becoming active and clear.

5. Chant "OM" for five minutes before bed. Do nothing else after. Just go to sleep.

Day 4

1. Mentally chant "OM" as you do the bellows breathing meditation for ten minutes

2. Do the dancing-legs-up-the-wall pose for five minutes.

3. Practice meditative eating with some or any of the chakra foods.

4. For five minutes, supercharge yourself with some indigo light.

5. Wrap up your day by contemplating an affirmation that calls to you the most.

Day 5

1. Mentally chant MMMM as you do a breathing meditation for ten minutes

2. Do the child's pose, puppy's pose, and legs up the wall pose for five minutes each.

3. Choose one affirmation to focus on from this book and contemplate it for ten minutes.

4. Meditate on a relevant crystal for ten minutes.

5. Wrap up your day by contemplating two affirmations that mean a lot to you.

Day 6

1. Pick one mantra and meditate on it for five minutes.

2. Breathe in indigo light for 15 minutes.

3. Chant "OM" for ten minutes as you do the chakra cleansing visualization.

4. Sit with a crystal and envision its energy as indigo light, enveloping you for five minutes.

5. Chant the "OM" mantra for 15 minutes, allowing it to take over you.

Day 7

1. Chant "MM" for five minutes, "MMMM" for five minutes, and "OM" for five more minutes.
2. Alternate between the child's pose, legs-up-the-wall pose, and puppy pose for 15 minutes.
3. Contemplate whatever it is that has been troubling you, and calmly affirm, "All is well."
4. Perform the bellows breath for five minutes while wearing a crystal and essential oil.
5. Wrap up your day by mentally chanting "OM," then "MMMM," and "OM" once more for five minutes each.

Crown Chakra Routine

Day 1

1. In the morning, chant "NG" for five minutes at least, 15 minutes tops.
2. Put a drop of essential oil on your collar or at the back of your ears after your shower.
3. Do some crown chakra breathing for just five minutes at noon, envisioning white light all around you.
4. Meditate for five minutes with a crown chakra crystal in hand while contemplating any of the affirmations.
5. At the end of the day, chant "NG" for five to 15 minutes.

Day 2

1. Chant "NG" first thing in the morning for five to 15 minutes.
2. For five minutes, visualize your crown chakra and do the chakra color breathing to get rid of any blockage you see in your mind's eye.
3. Pick one affirmation to contemplate for five minutes.
4. Eat something violet today, meditating on each bite as it goes down.
5. At the end of the day, chant a mantra that you deeply resonate with.

Day 3

1. Start your day by contemplating one of the affirmations given in this book. Take at least five minutes, at most 15 minutes.
2. Envelope yourself in a violet light to charge your chakra for five minutes.
3. Do the sipping breath while repeating the "NG" mantra in your mind.
4. Do the baby rabbit stand pose for just five minutes.
5. Wrap up your day by contemplating a different affirmation for five minutes.

Day 4

1. Chant "NG" at the start of your day for ten minutes.
2. Practice mindful eating with one of the white crown chakra foods.
3. Do the crocodile pose for five minutes.
4. Sit for 15 minutes, envisioning yourself being enveloped by bright, beautiful violet and white light.
5. End your day by repeating a mantra out loud to yourself while you fall asleep.

Day 5

1. Chant "NG" for 15 minutes to start your day.
2. Read all the affirmations for the chakra over and over for five minutes. Feel the words you say.
3. Work with some essential oil and sit and meditate on the smell and the way it makes you feel in the crown chakra area while doing the cooling breath.
4. Do the cow face pose while mentally chanting "NG" for five minutes.
5. Wrap up your day by chanting an affirmation as you fall asleep.

Day 6

1. Start by chanting "NG" for 15 minutes.
2. Go barefoot for a walk outside, and with each step, envision white light coming down from the sky, moving

down through the top of your head, and charging your crown chakra.

3. Eat a crown chakra meal mindfully.

4. Do the rabbit stand, crocodile, and cow face poses for just five minutes each, alternating between the three.

5. Go to bed chanting "NG" for 15 minutes. Do nothing else after. Just go to sleep.

Day 7

1. Start your day breathing in white light into your crown chakra for 15 minutes while mentally focusing on the mantra "NG."

2. Head outside and lie down on your back on the grass. Soak up the sky's energy.

3. Do the three yoga poses outlined in the book for this chakra, cycling back and forth for 15 minutes.

4. Do the sipping breath technique for ten minutes today.

5. Go to bed chanting "NG" as you fall asleep.

Notes

If you want to get actual results, you need to stay consistent with this and do this as methodically as you can while being open to whatever experiences will result from your efforts.

Extra: Quick Quiz — Which of My Chakras Are Out of Balance?

1. What is something that troubles you the most?
    a. Fear
    b. Guilt
    c. Shame
    d. Grief
    e. Dishonesty
    f. Delusions
    g. Attachments
2. What form of growth are you really into right now?
    a. Self-care
    b. Care for your body
    c. Self-empowerment
    d. Self-love
    e. Self-expression
    f. Journaling
    g. Mindfulness

3. Which color are you drawn to the most?
   a. Red
   b. Orange
   c. Yellow
   (d.) Green
   e. Blue
   f. Indigo
   g. Violet
4. Where do you tend to have the most issues?
   a. financial issues
   b. Problems with betrayal
   c. Fear of rejection
   d. Fear of being alone
   (e.) Fear of losing control
   f. Constant moodiness
   g. Fear of alienation
5. Which crystal are you most drawn to?
   c. Ruby
   d. Citrine
   e. Amber
   (f.) Emerald
   g. Lapis lazuli
   h. Purpurite
   i. Clear quartz
6. What foods are you most drawn to right now?
   c. Strawberries
   (d.) Oranges
   e. Bananas
   f. green grapes
   g. Blueberries
   h. Eggplant
   i. Celery

7. Which of the following sounds (bija mantras – or seed sounds) make you react noticeably?

    c. Lam

    d. Vam

    e. Ram

    f. Yam

    (g.) Ham

    h. Om

    i. Ng

8. What could you use the most in your life right now?

    c. Security

    d. Sensuality

    e. Power

    f. Love

    g. Truth

    (h.) Insight

    i. Wisdom

9. If you had to choose one out of all the options below, what would it be?

    c. To have

    d. To feel

    e. To act

    f. To love

    (g.) To be heard and to speak

    h. To see

    i. To know

10. Right now, what are you drawn to the most?

    c. Earth

    d. Fire

    e. Water

    (f.) Air

    g. Sound

h. Light

i. Thoughts

Each letter of the alphabet used to represent the options stands for the chakras in ascending order, from root to crown.

Question 1: Addresses what imbalance you're likely dealing with.

Question 2: This shows you're working on that issue, which means you're somehow aware of the chakra giving you issues.

Question 3: The color you're drawn to is likely the chakra you'll need to work on the most, and whatever gives you the most issues should show you further proof of what troubles you.

Question 4: Whatever aspect of life that plagues you the most should show you where your imbalance lies.

Question 5: You'll be drawn to the crystal that matches the chakra that needs the most work in your life.

Question 6: You're drawn to that food because that chakra likely needs some work.

Question 7: You're likely to react the most to the seed sound for the most imbalance or blocked chakra you have.

Question 8: This highlight what you need the most, which is connected to the correspondent imbalanced or inactive chakra.

Question 9: Your answer here is telling about what needs work.

Question 10: The element that you chose will likely be tied to what you're working on.

Obviously, not all your answers will match the others, but it could be a sign that you need to work on more than just one chakra. That's okay and nothing to be miffed about. Just do the outlined routines for each one or mix and match as needed. As long as you're consistent and show each chakra equal love, you'll get the results you seek.

Part 2: Chakra Yoga

The Ultimate Guide to Balancing, Awakening, and Healing Your Chakras Using Yoga Poses

Introduction

Yoga can help us achieve unity in the spiritual, physical, and mental aspects of our being. It forges a sense of alignment in all that we are and allows us to connect to the very essence of our existence. This is why you can think of yoga as a holistic healing method. Take the time to reflect on your thoughts and feelings when you need to tackle certain things. Do you easily get overwhelmed even when it comes to the most trivial tasks? Do you tend to feel lost and confused? Are your thoughts rather conflicting?

Our minds usually go back and forth between overthinking past events and worrying about the future. Feelings of anxiety, fear, desire, and anticipation take over most of the time. The solution here isn't to try and suppress your thoughts but to avert them. You can achieve that by redirecting your mind to the present moment, which is the ultimate goal of yoga. Regular yoga practice can allow you to cleanse and free your mind, soul, and body from pent-up stress and negative feelings and emotions. It can also help you relieve a ruffled mind. Yoga can help you achieve better mental clarity, flexibility, and physical balance. It undoubtedly gives you mental and physical strength and promotes optimal health and alertness. Your daily life will eventually reflect what you achieve on the mat regarding behavior, discipline, focus, and attention. It may not sound believable now. However, training yourself to breathe under the strain of performing yoga postures can also help you breathe better under pressure.

When you do yoga, you work at your own pace. You start learning to trust your body and believe you'll progress in time. Focusing on your efforts without comparing yourself to others' performance can influence how you approach all life situations. Instead of needing to match your success to that of others, you'll give it your all and solely focus on yourself. Detaching yourself from the outcomes can help you diminish your stress.

If you're reading this book, you're likely searching for ways to balance your chakras and awaken them. Fortunately, yoga happens to be an invaluable practice to help foster a smooth and stable flow of energy throughout the body. As we'll see, certain yoga postures resonate with specific chakras, allowing them to activate.

The health of your chakras is affected by your mental, physical, emotional, and spiritual well-being. A hindered energetic flow causes all sorts of impairments, further influencing your general health in these areas of your life. Being a holistic practice, yoga targets every aspect of your health, making it the ideal chakra healing and awakening practice.

Upon reading this book, you'll learn all about the chakra system and how it works. Chapters 3 through 9 are dedicated to balancing each of the seven chakras. Each chapter introduces a certain energy center and explains its function, the symptoms associated with the blockage of that chakra, what obstructs it in the first place, and what it feels like to have it activated and balanced. You'll also find a step-by-step yoga sequence you can follow to encourage the healing of that chakra. Chapter 10 will introduce you to other practices designed to further support your chakra balancing journey: using healing crystals and reciting affirmations. There, you'll find a 7-day yoga routine. Finally, you'll find a quiz that will help you determine which of your chakras needs healing.

Now that you know what lies ahead and what you stand to gain from these practices, let's delve into the world of spirituality and chakra yoga!

Chapter 1: What Are the Chakras?

Chakra symbols
https://pixabay.com/images/id-7182133/

If you are even remotely familiar with practices like yoga, reiki, or meditation, then you've probably heard of chakras, and you've also heard about how they can be blocked or over-activated. It doesn't necessarily mean you know precisely what a chakra is and how it can affect your overall health. This opening chapter will walk you through the different chakras, their location in the body, the purpose they serve, and how taking care of them can help boost your physical and spiritual well-being.

The Meaning of Chakra

The word chakra is Sanskrit for "disk" or "wheel," which denotes certain energy centers in your body. These energy centers are spread throughout different areas, and each wheel that spins energy corresponds to a specific bundle of nerves and major organs. If you envision little wheels spinning in different parts of your body, that's basically what the chakras are, except each one represents a specific set of physical and spiritual energies. The concept of a chakra is integral to philosophies that govern yogic and meditation practices, which can be found in other areas of Eastern medicine, such as acupuncture and reiki.

The first mention of the chakra system can be found in a sacred text, the Vedas, which indicates it originated in India between 1,500 and 500 B.C. Vedas are the very first literary records found in Sanskrit, and they are considered the most ancient scriptures of Hinduism. Furthermore, the spiritual texts indicate that the central purpose of the seven chakras is to work together in harmony, ultimately leading to a state called "prana," which denotes pure, healing energy that can be found within us and capable of keeping us happy and healthy. Before we deconstruct the meaning of the chakras, let's list them here and explain how they function.

Root Chakra

Even if you're not sure what chakras are just yet, chances are you've heard plenty about the root chakra - it tends to get called out a lot in the middle of a yoga or meditation session. The root chakra is located at the base of the spine, the pelvic floor, and the first three vertebrae.

The root chakra is conventionally seen as the foundation of your body. Therefore, when it's in balance, your foundation is on solid ground, and you feel supported. Deeply tied to a sense of security, people need a balanced root chakra to feel that they can survive. Survival here is meant both in the emotional sense and in a deeply tangible way. Your capacity to ensure the most basic needs, such as a roof over your head, food, and water, while also taking care of your emotional needs, is tied to your root chakra. When you feel vulnerable or insecure, then your root chakra isn't in a good place, and you may need to unblock it before you can feel safe again. Those with a balanced chakra will worry less and have fewer issues with an ambient form of anxiety, which has become rather widespread.

If you're wondering whether your root chakra is blocked, conduct a mental check, and make a list of whatever is ailing you. If your afflictions run the gamut of anxiety disorders, you have frequent nightmares, and you notice physical issues affecting your colon, bladder, or experience pain in your lower back, legs, or feet, *your root chakra is likely blocked.*

The root chakra is associated with the color red, and its element is earth.

Sacral Chakra

There tends to be less of a buzz around the sacral chakra, but it is second in line and has another essential purpose in our lives. It is located just above the pubic bone, below the navel. In terms of its central function, this chakra houses emotions, desires, passions, and whatever gives us pleasure, both emotionally and physically. It tends to be associated with joy and is often considered the body's creative and sexual center.

As you can probably imagine, a balanced sacral chakra will leave you feeling wonderful. You'll be open, friendly with others, and experience a sense of fulfillment. Your feelings of wellness and joy will be enhanced, feeling appreciative of your body and allowing you to express yourself creatively. These are all good things we all strive towards.

When the sacral chakra is imbalanced or blocked, you'll feel the opposite of everything listed above. Creative inspiration will feel so far that it might look as though it never hit you. At the same time, you may be struggling with various forms of sexual dysfunction, depression, or even find yourself resorting to addictive behaviors. These are all profound warning signs that something may be off, and you need to rebalance this chakra as soon as possible.

The sacral chakra is associated with the color orange, and it manifests itself with the element of water.

Solar Plexus Chakra

After that comes the solar plexus chakra, which sits between the navel and the ribcage area. It helps regulate anything to do with metabolic and digestive functions and stomach-related ailments. It is arguably the most physical of all chakras, and it can wreak havoc on your entire system.

At the same time, the solar plexus chakra can affect your sense of self-esteem and willpower. Any commitment to a specific project or person may be compromised when this chakra is off-balance. So, yes, it deeply affects your physicality, but it can also compromise a core sense of self. This shouldn't be entirely surprising to those who already suffer in some way from digestive issues like IBS - once something affects your stomach, your self-esteem begins to nosedive since they are more intimately connected than you'd think.

So, you'll know if your solar plexus chakra is blocked or imbalanced if you are experiencing low confidence levels and have difficulty making decisions. Also, if you suddenly feel a loss of control and a surge in anger, you're suffering from a problem with this chakra. In more extreme cases, you may feel apathetic, struggle to get to appointments on time, and your work performance will plummet. Worse yet, you may go to another extreme: you may have bouts of hyperactive energy and an almost egomaniacal level of overconfidence. These indicate that you are out of touch with yourself and need to feel grounded and more authentic.

The solar plexus chakra is associated with the color yellow, and the element of fire represents it.

Heart Chakra

The heart chakra is central, ruling over the heart and thymus gland, affecting the endocrine and lymphatic system and the lungs and breasts. This fourth chakra represents the intersection wherein physical and spiritual needs can be met. Ultimately, it symbolizes love. The heart chakra is important because it helps with major spiritual issues such as forgiveness, one's capacity to be of service to the community, and healing powers. You'll feel grounded, loved, and compassionate towards yourself and those around you when you have a well-balanced chakra. You'll emit lots of good vibes to such an extent that people may feel its contagious effects simply by being near year.

When the heart chakra is blocked, you'll mostly experience feelings of grief, jealousy, betrayal, and perhaps even hatred. Everything is heightened, but not in a good way. Likewise, if the heart chakra is underactive, it may result in you shutting down emotionally as a way to protect yourself. Things like forgiveness and moving past slights will seem like a tall order, and you can be consumed by a wave of sadness on most days - even when it seems as though you're as cold as a fish to others. This type of behavior deeply affects relationships, and your romantic and platonic partnerships will suffer tremendously.

If your heart chakra is overactive, you may be feeling lovey-dovey all the time, leading you to engage with situations that leave you vulnerable. Suddenly, boundaries evaporate, and your capacity to care for your needs in different relationships takes a backseat, leading to dissatisfaction and resentment in the long run.

The heart chakra is associated with the colors green and pink, and the element of air represents it.

Throat Chakra

The throat chakra is responsible for your throat, thyroid, jaw, neck, mouth, larynx, tongue, and parathyroid. It affects your capacity to speak for yourself and allows for proper expression. So, if you're wondering if your throat chakra is balanced, ask yourself: Are you able to communicate your deepest thoughts and feelings properly? Is communication hard or relatively easy? If it's the former, your throat chakra is most likely off.

The throat chakra is one of the purely spiritual chakras, and it manifests itself rather differently. As we've covered so far, the lower chakras are more physical and therefore manifest themselves in more physical ways. Not so for the throat chakra. As previously mentioned, it's mostly concerned with communication, so when it's underactive, you won't be able to express your thoughts or feelings easily. You may feel avoidant and not want to speak for fear of feeling vulnerable or having others judge you. You may also experience trouble concentrating, jeopardizing your sense of groundedness.

So, while the throat chakra is deeply spiritual, it may have a placebo effect on you physically. You may find yourself unable to speak, almost as though you're suffering from a sore throat. Tension headaches are also bound to occur since your inability to express yourself will leave you feeling quite stressed.

On the other hand, if your throat chakra is overactive, you may be talking too much, which is where the expression "word vomit" comes into play. It can be a slippery slope since people around you'll find you overly domineering in discussions, and you may even come across as a judgmental and obnoxious person.

The throat chakra is associated with the color blue, and it is manifested in the element of ether.

Third Eye Chakra

The third eye tends to get confused with expressions like "the mind's eye," and it's not far off. The third eye is located right between the eyebrows, and it rules over certain organs such as the pituitary gland, eyes, lower part of the brain, and the head.

"Third eye" could seem to be a bit of a misnomer since, technically, this is the sixth chakra. It governs your sense of intuition, which is where the idea of harnessing your psychic abilities comes from when we sometimes talk about the mind's eye or the third eye. In addition, the third eye is responsible for all the things between you and the world around you. When this chakra is balanced, you can cut through all the noise and rid yourself of any illusions, allowing you to feel grounded and clear-eyed about everything.

If your third eye chakra is blocked, you're probably having trouble harnessing your intuition and trusting yourself. You may even find yourself unable to learn new skills suddenly. This chakra is also tied to the lower chakras; your third eye will also be affected if those are blocked. This can cause you to be more introverted than usual, or you may be extra judgmental of others and incapable of listening to other people.

An underactive chakra may cause you to over-intellectualize everything without being able to pay attention to how you're feeling. This leads to feelings of overwhelm and exhaustion since not being able to trust your gut and reverting to seeing everything through a purely practical prism will leave you feeling distrustful and anxious.

When the third eye chakra is blocked, you'll experience a wide range of emotional problems, the chief of which are depression and anxiety. These could lead to physical symptoms like nausea, constant headaches, and perhaps even migraines. Interestingly, if your third eye chakra is overactive, then you may find yourself overly imaginative, if that's even possible. You'll be daydreaming a lot, experience vivid nightmares, and may feel your clairvoyant skills becoming so active that you'll inevitably be overwhelmed.

The third eye chakra is associated with the color indigo and is manifested within the element of light.

Crown Chakra

The last of the seven chakras, the crown chakra, is located at the very top of your head. It is considered the center of all enlightenment, and it rules the spiritual connection to your higher self, others, and the divine power you believe in. When your crown chakra is balanced, you'll have laser focus and feel your consciousness expand. However, when it is underactive, you'll automatically feel restless and numb since you won't feel connected or grounded. It also results in feeling that you have no clear direction in life and lack purpose.

In stark contrast, an overactive crown chakra will induce an overwhelming desire for material possessions, accumulating many things to fulfill a large void left in one's life. This could lead to greed, craven materialism, and arrogance since there is a lack of connection with the world around you.

The crown chakra is associated with the color violet and, unlike all the other chakras, does not manifest itself within an element.

A Holistic Effort

While each chakra has a specific role in your physical and spiritual life, they work together like a complex, well-oiled machine. If one is off-balance, you'll run into trouble with the rest. For example, you cannot have a blocked root chakra and expect your heart chakra to be working optimally. You're probably sitting on plenty of negative emotions and maybe even feeling a bit of physical pain. Things tend to worsen if you have more than one of the chakras blocked. So, if you're finding that you have two or more chakras blocked or overactive, the following chapters will provide you with some much-needed guidance. There are a few things you can look for to achieve more balance in life, and these practices will be incredibly useful to keep in your arsenal for years to come.

Chapter 2: Introduction to Chakra Yoga

Many of us are familiar with the term "yoga," but do we really know what yoga is? Statements like "yoga is all about posture" or "yoga is a religious practice" are too common, but these are some of the many misconceptions about yoga. Although it originated in Hinduism, yoga isn't a religious practice since no religious rituals like praying or worshiping deities are involved. Yoga is a practice that focuses on the body, mind, and spirit, and in which many people find peacefulness and a sense of spirituality.

Another misconception is that yoga is about stretching or adopting the right body posture. In truth, yoga is more than just physical exercise. Although posture and stretching are central aspects, the physical side is what gets us into yoga and isn't the practice itself. Various schools and branches of yoga involve elements like breathing exercises and meditation techniques. Learning about what yoga is really about will encourage you to incorporate it into your daily routine and reap its countless benefits.

What Is Yoga?

Yoga poses.
https://unsplash.com/photos/F2qh3vjz6Jk

Yoga is an ancient practice whose origins can be traced back to Indian culture. However, it was only in the 20th century that it became popular in the western world. Yoga was initially a spiritual practice, but it has become an exercise that can improve your physical strength, flexibility, balance, and coordination. It also relaxes your mind and body and benefits your overall well-being. This is only a small part of what this practice offers. Among the many aspects of yoga in the United States, it mainly focuses on meditation, body posture, and breathing techniques.

Yoga is derived from the Sanskrit word *Yuj*, which means "to unite." This is because, at its core, yoga was a practice designed to unite the spirit, mind, body, universal consciousness, and individual self with one another. Once this unity is achieved, you experience a spiritual awakening.

This practice has been popular for thousands of years and has gained huge popularity in the west, and for a good reason. You should give yoga a chance if you want to connect with your body, improve your physical strength, posture, sleep, and experience the many benefits of breathing exercises and meditation. Many people who have made yoga a part of their lifestyle have noticed great improvements in their well-being. You, too, can reap these benefits by practicing for 10 minutes every day. This small window you'll dedicate to yoga daily can make you feel like a whole new person.

The Different Types of Yoga

There are different types of yoga out there, and each one offers something unique to the body, mind, or spirit.

Hatha Yoga

Hatha yoga is the most popular branch in the western world. "*Ha*" is the Sanskrit word for the sun, while "*Tha*" is the moon. "Hatha" is considered an umbrella term for all styles that focus on the physical aspect of yoga. It includes various elements of yoga-like posture (asana), breathing exercises (pranayama), and mudra (hand gestures). Hatha yoga helps balance the seven chakras and create harmony throughout your body. This style is ideal for beginners since it involves gentler poses and a slower pace.

Ashtanga Yoga

Ashtanga is a Sanskrit word that means "eight limb path," It became popular in the early 1900s. This typically involves more intense and challenging postures, making it suitable for intermediate to advanced yogis. If you want to practice Ashtanga yoga, you should first familiarize yourself with its 6 sets of sequences. This exercise is better suited to athletes since it is physically demanding, also offering mental and physical benefits like improving mindfulness, endurance, and flexibility.

Bikram Yoga

Bikram yoga is named after its founder, Bikram Choudhury. However, after Bikram was accused of sexual harassment, the name became tainted. This is when a similar exercise inspired by Bikram yoga came to be and is known as hot yoga.

Bikram yoga involves 26 postures and two breathing exercises. It differs from the previous two types as it must be performed in a closed room with a temperature of 105°F and 40% humidity. This essentially mimics the Indian climate where its founder is from.

Vinyasa Yoga

Vinyasa derives from two Sanskrit words meaning "to place in a special way." Like Ashtanga, it is another more suitable exercise for athletic movements. Vinyasa yoga involves body posture and breathing exercises derived from Ashtanga yoga.

Iyengar Yoga

Iyengar yoga was named after its founder, B.K.S. Iyengar. This type involves specific movements and props like cushions or blankets to achieve proper posture and alignment. Unlike other mentioned types, Iyengar yoga involves a slower pace, much like Hatha. However, it requires great concentration since you'll hold poses for a long period. Many people who have practiced this type after an injury have praised Iyengar yoga for helping them through their recovery.

Restorative Yoga

Restorative yoga is similar to Iyengar yoga. It was developed by one of B.K.S. Iyengar's students, American yoga instructor Judith Hanson. This exercise essentially focuses on cleansing the mind and relaxing the body.

Yin Yoga

Yin yoga involves slow-paced sitting postures and stretches. You can also incorporate meditation into this practice to help you achieve inner clarity and peace.

Chakra Yoga

Yoga and chakras are deeply connected. As mentioned previously, chakras are the energy centers in the body. These centers can sometimes be blocked or unbalanced, manifest in mental or physical symptoms like anxiety or digestive issues. So, how can we remedy this problem and restore our chakras? The answer lies in yoga.

Various yoga forms focus on unblocking the chakras. Yoga chakra usually includes meditation, posture, breathing exercises, and hand gestures. Each chakra has its own yoga techniques, breathing exercises, and meditation techniques that can bring balance to the chakra, which we will discuss in the coming chapters.

While each chakra responds to various exercises, yoga positively impacts your whole body. When you practice a yoga exercise to unblock a chakra, it can balance and heal your other chakras, different parts of your body, and mind. Yoga harmonizes the body and creates alignments through its different postures. This can, in turn, bring balance to your subtle body, where the chakras exist.

The movements in chakra yoga work to release the energy stuck in your body. When we experience these stale energies, yoga postures bring relief and fresher energy to your body thanks to breathing exercises and various postures. Chakras and yoga are both old concepts, so it only makes sense for one to rely on the other for healing. For instance, Hatha yoga postures help unblock the chakras since it works on aligning your spine, which is where the chakra energies flow. This helps restore the body's physical and mental balance. Hatha yoga is often compared to Kundalini yoga since both share many similarities, including opening the seven chakras.

What Is Kundalini?

Kundalini, or Kundalini Shakti, is the life-force energy located at the base of your spine and the Meldhuara (the root chakra), the first of the seven chakras. Think of the chakras as doorways to your perceptions. Now, what would happen if they were blocked? How would the Kundalini energy flow? By practicing Kundalini yoga, you release the energy stuck in this part of your body, so it passes through the seven chakras. As a result, we experience positive emotions and energies.

Kundalini is everything that you are, everything experienced by your consciousness. Kundalini is Sanskrit for "coiled snake," which describes the stagnant energy near your root chakra. Kundalini yoga includes yoga poses, meditation, mantras, and various breathing exercises. Yogis use Hatha physical poses and add their own breathing exercises and mantras. Combining different aspects of yoga is called *kriya*, a Sanskrit word meaning "action." When you practice kriya, you reach Kundalini awareness, which is awakening your consciousness and awareness.

However, Kundalini doesn't come from yoga. While we don't know exactly where it originated, it was mentioned in ancient Indian texts. The Kundalini yoga we practice today is inspired by various yogic principles to reach the divine and feel its presence in our minds. This is the phenomenon known as the Kundalini awakening. We all have Kundalini energy, but we aren't necessarily experiencing Kundalini awareness.

Awakening the Kundalini can transform your life and fill it with joy and happiness. For this reason, when one or more of your chakras is blocked, it can hinder the energy flow and interfere with your Kundalini awakening. Simply put, Kundalini is a process concerned with the energy flow in your body. If the energy is stagnant, it remains in the base of your spine (root chakra). Kundalini yoga is what gets this energy moving. This sounds good, doesn't it? Well, it depends.

At times, this energy flow is also referred to as the movement of the snake) can have negative consequences. It can cause major changes in our lives, which, if we aren't ready for it, can be a highly unpleasant experience. For instance, when your Kundalini is awakened, you may make big decisions, such as breaking up with your partner. While this might have been the right choice for you, it wasn't something you were ready for. Something in you has changed or awakened, so to handle these sudden changes, you'll first need to do some soul-searching to make peace with this new experience or awakening. Whether or not these changes are for the best, we may be unable to handle them, so we will need to rekindle this feeling of awareness first.

When deciding to awaken Kundalini, you must be aware of the path your prana (life-force energy) will take to enter and exit your subtle body. Practicing kriya can go both ways, in that you can either feel joyful and relaxed afterward or triggered. This exercise aims to challenge you and make your inner demons resurface. This doesn't make this practice harmful. On the contrary, it makes you aware of what's holding you back in life to face it to grow and become a better version of yourself. For that reason, Kundalini yoga is considered one of the most powerful types of yoga.

Kundalini yoga doesn't only borrow from Hatha yoga but from Raja yoga (the practice of mental power and mediation), Shakti yoga (expression of power), and Bhakti yoga (the practice of devotion) as well.

Signs of Kundalini Awakening

- You become more creative and empathetic
- You begin to see your life from a new perspective
- You are no longer driven by your ego or the material world
- You reach a feeling of clarity that gives you the courage to make the necessary changes in your life
- Your past traumas no longer impact your life
- Your crown chakra is unblocked
- You are more focused, and your thoughts are more organized
- You feel one with your surroundings and have love and compassion for everything that exists in this world

Now, if your chakras are blocked, and the Kundalini is unable to flow, you may experience:

- Trouble sleeping
- Body spasms
- Feeling hot

Hatha Yoga vs. Kundalini Yoga

With its rising popularity over the last few decades, Kundalini yoga is often compared to Hatha yoga. While Hatha yoga is more physical, Kundalini yoga focuses more on meditation and mantras. Both types of yoga share quite a few similarities like body poses, techniques, breathing exercises, and some mantras. If you happen to attend sessions for both, you'll notice some differences, mainly because the classes are structured this way.

Hatha and Kundalini complement each other since Kundalini is more focused on the spiritual aspect of yoga, so it borrows its physical poses from Hatha, whereas Hatha borrows its mantras from Kundalini. Kundalini yoga can provide you with a more spiritual experience, while Hatha is best for those who want to work on their physical bodies.

Different Aspects of Yoga Practice

Now that we know the different types of yoga and understand what Chakra yoga is, let's go over the essential components of yoga practice.

Pranayama (Breathing)

Pranayama encompasses the various breathing techniques you practice during yoga and meditation. The purpose of these exercises is to get rid of the physical or emotional obstacles in your body to clear the way for your prana to flow easily.

Although breathing keeps us alive, we often take it for granted. However, the stress of our everyday life coupled with unhealthy habits can create energetic obstacles that may impact our breathing. As a result, we develop breathing patterns that inherently restrict energy flow throughout our bodies.

We free up our breathing and prana to flow easily through our chakras by practicing breathing exercises. This makes us feel energized, more relaxed, and positive. It also clears our chakras, brings clarity to the body, improves our physical health, and creates harmony between our spirit, mind, and body.

Asanas (Poses)

Asana is a Sanskrit word meaning "seat," representing the physical aspect of yoga. Many people identify yoga with Asana, especially if they are unfamiliar with the other aspects of yoga. Yoga was originally more of a spiritual practice than a physical one. Although yoga has a predominantly physical dimension these days, it isn't necessarily considered yoga. In other words, yoga requires specific and highly-calibrated poses, so if you simply sit in a yoga pose without considering the spiritual dimension, you aren't practicing yoga. Other aspects must be considered as well, like mediation and breathing exercise. All in all, Asana allows you to practice yoga, not just perform the practice itself.

There are many benefits to Asana yoga, including post-injury recovery, increasing endurance, improving balance and flexibility, lowering inflammation, and improving physical strength.

Meditation and Relaxation

As you're certainly aware, meditation is another central tenet of yoga. You can meditate without practicing yoga and practice yoga without meditation. While the word "meditate" means to reflect or ponder on something, it is the state of pure consciousness in yoga. It helps you become mindful so you can live in the present moment. Meditation also enables you to connect with your body, mind, and the world. There are great health benefits to meditation, like reduced stress and anxiety, increased creativity and self-awareness, groundedness, and providing you with emotional stability.

Benefits of Making Chakra Yoga Part of Your Daily Routine

Since yoga isn't something you do once and wait for your chakras to open, it should be incorporated into your routine. To reap the many benefits of yoga and help open your chakra, you should practice yoga every day. Practicing daily yoga will:

- Point out your weaknesses, whether physical, mental, or emotional, and highlight your strengths so you can work on areas that need improvement
- Balance your seven chakras and help you reap the benefits of opened chakras
- Improve your well-being and put you in a state of harmony

Tips to Get You Started

If you haven't practiced yoga before, you are probably wondering how to get started. Don't worry; we have you covered with these helpful tips to awaken the yogi inside of you:

- Yoga creates harmony within and between your body, mind, and spirit. You are still a beginner, so give yourself the chance to evolve naturally and focus on what you'll gain from the practice rather than what it looks like on social media
- Always focus on your breathing

- Start by learning simple, basic yoga poses and work your way up from there
- Enroll in a yoga class and work with a registered instructor
- Opt for comfortable clothes and a non-slip mat
- Always practice in a quiet place free of distractions
- Set intentions before every session
- Be consistent and persevere!

Make Yoga a Habit

Adopting yoga as a habit will enable you to reap its great benefits and transform your life for the better. Now, how can you incorporate yoga into your busy schedule?

- Set time every day and make it a part of your daily schedule. Wake up 20 or 30 minutes early to practice yoga in peace, with no distractions. Practicing yoga in the morning will set the tone for the rest of the day.
- Practice at the same time every day
- Set a comfortable, quiet, well-ventilated, and well-lit space at home to stay motivated and practice every day
- Set a reminder on your phone for practice to avoid missing a session
- There will be days when you won't feel like practicing. That's all right. Developing a habit isn't easy, and it will take time to get used to it. Don't beat yourself up if you miss practice one day. There is always tomorrow.

Yoga can do wonders for every aspect of your life. It is one of the best methods to open up your seven chakras. Include yoga as part of your lifestyle, and watch your life transform in incredible ways.

Chapter 3: Ground Your Root Chakra

Also known as Muladhara in Sanskrit, the root chakra can be found at the base of the spine. This is the first chakra, serving as a base for all the chakras located above it. To balance energy flow throughout your entire body, you'd have to start at the Muladhara. The element of the root chakra is Earth, and it is associated with the qualities of inertia, initiative, and enthusiasm.

In the womb, humans start developing their spinal cord from the bottom, where the root chakra is located, moving up to the Crown chakra. The root chakra is closely tied to our instincts, making it essential for our survival. It is responsible for our fight or flight response at the most basic level. The Muladhara is also the core of our sense of security and balance since it comes into play at birth when it works to help us understand the sudden shift in the environment and what we're doing here.

Besides our basic needs like food, water, and shelter, we each have a unique understanding of what it takes to feel grounded. That said, the root chakra represents the things in life that make us feel that way. This applies to our physical needs and commands our need for safety, connection, and emotional fulfillment.

The root chakra is the basis of our Qi, Prana, or Kundalini Shakti (life force energy). The Muladhara is where the ultimate life force energy resides, in its dormant state. When balanced and open, the root chakra allows the dormant energy to be activated and flow to replenish the other six chakras, elevating you to a higher state of consciousness. The level of consciousness awakened at the activated root chakra is enthusiasm. This quality, which tends to be overlooked, is behind all actions we willingly take. It serves as a source of support and helps us approach life optimistically and vivaciously.

Without enthusiasm, life lacks meaning. We become bored, inactive, stagnant, and submerged by feelings of loss and purposelessness. When the life energy comes back and hits the root chakra from the crown chakra, feelings of inertia and passivity are evoked. Each chakra links to a negative and positive quality, depending on where the life energy is coming from and where it's headed to. This is why it's important to maintain balance in the entire chakra system, starting at the root and working your way up to ensure your physical, mental, and emotional well-being.

Think of the root chakra as the hub where self-confidence and esteem, virtue and integrity, and a sense of safety and belonging are developed, nurtured, and maintained.

Upon reading this chapter, you'll understand what a blocked root chakra looks like and the physical, emotional, and spiritual symptoms that this issue brings along. You'll find out the common causes for a Muladhara imbalance and learn some signs that it is balanced or active. This chapter also includes step-by-step instructions for a yoga sequence you can practice regularly to activate your root chakra.

The Functions of the Muladhara

The Muladhara, which serves as the "root" of the body, acts as a spiritual and physical support system. Not only does it help us maintain a strong spiritual connection with the Earth and the physical world, but it supports the body's bone structure as well. A balanced root chakra is vital to our mental, spiritual, and physical health. When this chakra gets blocked, all others fall out of balance.

What Causes a Blocked Root Chakra?

The root chakra carries ancestral memories, including generational traumas and years of hardships. The Muladhara is believed to be the gateway through which we interact and connect with our ancestors and their spiritual energies. Therefore, we are also exposed to their successes and the challenges and ordeals they experienced in their own lifetime. Past disasters like war and fatal accidents are passed down from one generation to the other, resulting in behavioral patterns that are both unconscious and unhelpful. In other words, the Muladhara carries the karmas of our previous and present lifetimes.

It comes as no surprise that our own upbringing influences the health of the root chakra. These ancestral memories also converge with our own life experiences. Everyone inevitably faces their fair share of troubles, risking an imbalance at some point in life. For example, an individual's ability to trust may have been hindered by neglectful parents. In that case, their trust issues will affect their sense of inner security, which is closely tied to the root chakra.

The root chakra is where the vital life energy resides, dormant. Fortunately, you can awaken it by practicing a wide range of healthy physical and spiritual exercises. These include partaking in prayers, meditating, or practicing asanas and pranayama. When you activate the Muladhara, you'll feel a shift in your mental, physical, emotional, and spiritual health. You'll be more grounded and, therefore, more self-confident. Doing so will also help you build a strong foundation for activating the chakras above, which will be our subject of interest throughout the following chapters.

An Imbalanced Root Chakra

Suppose you're somewhat educated about the chakra system. In that case, you'll be able to tell if one of your chakras is blocked or seemingly out of balance. You'll feel some obstruction or tension build up in a certain part of your body. You may receive certain comments about being "off" in one way or another. While you may feel compelled to do something about it right away, the best cure starts with patience. To re-align your chakras, you must take the time to connect with your body and listen to what it wants to communicate to you. Make it your mission to notice how you feel in all aspects, whether mentally, emotionally, physically, or spiritually.

When the root chakra falls out of balance or becomes blocked, your motivation and willingness to move forward are severely affected. You no longer feel the joy and essence of life, and you may lose your sense of direction and struggle to experience pleasure in what you normally do. When our Muladhara is stagnant, we are no longer in touch with our purpose and typically feel like we don't belong.

All these emotions give rise to numerous unwanted symptoms. We feel insecure, unsafe, and restless when the ultimate life force energy returns to its dormant state. People who struggle with an imbalanced root chakra may experience mental issues like depression, whose most severe manifestations can cause suicidal thoughts, inexplicable rage and anger, feelings of resentment, anxiety, and low self-esteem. They also tend to be pessimistic, disoriented, and unable to focus.

An imbalance in the root chakra happens due to a downflow of energy. This will make you feel overly tired, lazy, and sluggish. These symptoms may manifest as more serious physical conditions that range from arthritis or back pain to constipation.

These symptoms and the innate sense of instability and insecurity can be very overwhelming. An imbalanced root chakra makes it impossible to garner one's inner strength to go on about life. It impacts our life and well-being on every level. This is why we need to work on the foundation and begin the root chakra healing journey to achieve free-flowing energies and a positive outlook on life.

Physical Symptoms of a Blocked Root Chakra

- Lower back issues and pains
- Prostate problems
- Unintentional weight gain or loss
- Constipation and other bladder problems

- Pelvic pain
- Problems with the left arm, foot, or leg
- Incontinence
- Colon problems
- Cramping
- Sluggishness
- Inflammation

Mental Symptoms of a Blocked Root Chakra

- Anxiety disorders
- A lack of focus and concentration
- Depression
- A sense of lethargy
- Diminished self-esteem
- Eating disorders
- Panic attacks

What Does a Balanced Root Chakra Feel Like

With a balanced root chakra, we feel present and in touch with our surroundings. We can offer our undivided attention to a given task without feeling distracted. You'll notice that you're more engaged in conversations and actively listen to others. A balanced root chakra will allow you to let go of the past, ease your worries about the future, and focus on the present. You can let go of feelings like shame, fear, and guilt, ultimately holding you back. You live life without obsession over expectations and certain outcomes, and therefore don't waste your time daydreaming about all that could be.

A balanced root chakra will keep you grounded in your own energy. You are fully aware of your own thoughts, feelings, wants, and needs, so you're not easily influenced by what other people do or say. You're no longer worried about what people think of you or how they feel toward you. You can maintain your sense of balance under potentially stressful or anxiety-triggering circumstances.

Healthy relationships and deep, genuine connections also form when our root chakra is balanced. We are confident in our right to be loved and supported and can seek help from our ancestors. When we're rooted, we are aligned with our physical body and its sensations. This alignment allows us to listen to our body and understand what it's trying to tell us. A balanced root chakra allows us to treat ourselves with compassion and forgiveness. One of the blocked root chakra symptoms is numbness or desensitization, which can be overcome by activating the Muladhara.

Since the root chakra is deeply associated with our groundedness and connection with the Earth, it is most balanced when we're in tune with Mother Nature. Connecting with nature fulfills numerous aspects of our being. At the very basic level, we experience relief from anxiety, which corresponds to wind energy, and better anger management, which is linked to fire energy. This is because a balanced root chakra sparks the realization of how air, fire, water, light, ice, darkness, and space all affect our physical and mental being. This means we start paying more attention to how our surroundings and the changing seasons affect our body, so we adjust our lifestyle, workout habits, diets, and self-care routines accordingly. For instance, if your root chakra is balanced. You may notice that you usually develop seasonal depression around wintertime. This way, you can take preventative measures to keep your energy intact. You may also notice that you tend to get lazy at certain times of the year, in which case you'll make your exercise routine more interesting or less demanding.

A balanced Muladhara allows you to feel that you truly belong. You can see things falling into place and witness your sense of safety is no longer compromised. You're driven, focused, and gratuitous. You're faithful that everything works out for the best, and don't fear the unknown. This is because an active root chakra works to heighten your intuition.

An activated Muladhara makes you more efficient and focused. It helps you stay organized and eliminates feelings of disarray. You can feel and see balance in your home and professional life. You are also more logical and rational and are more aligned with common sense. You aren't stuck in the planning phase and feel ready to take action right away, which helps you grow further and accomplish great things in life. You're not fixated on fears about financial stability and career goals. Although it can be terrifying to many people, stillness does not upset rooted individuals. Rather, they view it as an opportunity to listen to their intuition.

Yoga Sequence for the Muladhara

When you practice yoga regularly, you'll experience a positive shift in your energy. This practice can help you flush out the toxins in your body and cleanse it. This yoga sequence starts with simple sitting poses and slowly increases in complexity. We encourage you to focus on your breaths and how your body feels as it moves while performing the following poses.

Prasarita Balasana - Wide Child Pose

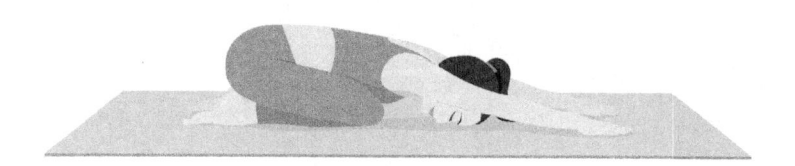

Wide child pose.

1. Sit down at the center of the mat in a simple Vajrasana pose. Keep your legs tucked beneath you and your hands on your thighs. Push your shoulders back and keep your back straight.

2. Close your eyes and breathe for a few moments, paying attention to your bodily sensations and how the air feels as it fills up and exits your lungs.
3. Inhale and push your knees wider apart, allowing your hips to touch the floor. Sit down comfortably between your legs and heels, pausing for a few moments to adjust and breathe.
4. Inhale while raising your hands above your head, extending your spine in the process. As you exhale, move your torso forward and towards the floor. Stretch out your hands, resting them on the floor, bringing your face close to the ground.
5. Stay in this pose for 12 slow and balanced breaths.

Masalana - Garland Pose

Garland pose.

1. Taking it from the Wide Child Pose, slowly raise your torso upwards and come up into a seated position.
2. Inhale and rise to your feet. Squat down and place your elbows between your thighs. Join the palms of your hands in a Namaste, pushing your thighs outwards in the process.
3. Sit in this pose for around 12 breaths, and bring your awareness to your body and breathing. Make sure your thighs are widened to their maximum capacity. Pay attention to your stretched lower back and hips.

Dandasana - Staff Pose

Dandasana.

Jemasty, CC BY-SA 3.0 <https://creativecommons.org/licenses/by-sa/3.0>, via Wikimedia Commons: https://commons.wikimedia.org/wiki/File:Dandasana_yoga_posture.jpg

1. Assume a seated position and stretch out your legs entirely in front of you. Sit straight and extend your spins while keeping your hips pushed firmly onto the floor. Close your eyes and feel this connection at the foundation of your spine.
2. Sit in this pose for 8 breaths. You may feel inclined to tense your body. However, you should try to relax and ease yourself into this position.

Paschimottanasana - Seated Forward Bend Pose

Seated forward bend.

1. Stay seated with your legs extended in front of you and inhale as you bring your hands over your head. As you exhale, move your arms forward and down, and reach for your feet. Allow your torso to flex in the process.
2. Feel the stretch at the base of your spine as you stay in this pose for at least 14 slow and steady breaths.

Baddha Hasta Uttanasana - Dangling Pose

RAG DOLL
Dangling Pose

Dangling pose.

1. From the squatted pose in Masalana, inhale as you bring your torso upwards with your entire weight shifted on your feet and legs. Your torso should fold at your hips, and your hands should dangle in front of your legs.

2. Interlock your arms at the elbows and close your face and chest towards your thighs. Flex your thighs at your hips as much as you can.
3. You'll feel a lot of pressure on your core and shoulder muscles. Now, consciously shift your awareness to your lower back, hips, and the base of your spine.
4. You should feel a deep stretch in the new area of focus. Keep yourself relaxed as you stay there for 8 breaths.

Utkatasana - Chair Pose

Chair pose.

1. Inhale and move your arms over your head. Slowly and carefully bend your knees in the process.
2. Contract your abdominal muscles and the muscles around the pelvis as much as possible.
3. Hold this pose for around 6 breaths as you focus on maintaining a steady breathing pattern. If you can, hold it for longer.

Parivrtta Utkatasana - Revolved Chair Pose

Revolved chair pose.

1. Keep your knees bent and exhale while twisting your torso to your right side. Join your hands in a Namaste, placing your palms on the outside of your right knee.
2. Move your elbow to the outside of your right knee, slowly twisting your body and moving your head to look upwards.
3. Focus on tightening your pelvic and abdominal muscles.
4. Hold this pose for 6 breaths. Make sure to twist deeper, further tightening your pelvic floor and lower back muscles with each breath you take.

Ultimately, the Muladhara forges a connection between the external, physical world and the energy system within us. When in an optimal state, our root chakra is what gives us the boost we need to get up in the morning, create, have kids, and make the most out of life. As we've seen, the root chakra also helps us build a connection with the Earth. This sense of groundedness or being "rooted" is what makes us feel secure. We all thrive on feeling safe and balanced, as it is naturally our topmost priority and instinct. Without this feeling, our energies will fail to flow freely and effectively. We won't feel motivated to carry on forward, or at least optimistically, in life. We'll learn how to unblock your sacral chakra in the upcoming chapter.

Chapter 4: Unblock Your Sacral Chakra

The sacral chakra, which comes second in the chakra system, sits right below the navel at the perineum. Its Sanskrit name Svadhisthana suggests this is where we are essentially "established." If you look up the symbol for this chakra, you'll see an orange illustration with six petals around multiple circles in the center. These circles depict birth, death, and rebirth, life cycles. Looking closer, you'll also notice a moon-crescent shape. This figure represents the relationship between the moon phases and the water tides. It is also supposed to remind us of the association between the concept of creativity and the moon phases. In general, the symbols and the colors used to represent the chakras reflect their vibrations.

The sacral chakra corresponds to the water element, the kidneys, and the sex organs. Many people believe this energy center to be ruled by the Hindu goddess, Parvati, as she is associated with power, fidelity, and fertility. These qualities are deeply linked to the Svadhisthana.

Besides these virtues, the sacral chakra also links to creativity, as inferred from the symbol and sensuality. This chakra is mainly concerned with the delivery of feelings of pleasure. Its function is to guarantee the enjoyment of life. When activated, we experience nurturing and harmonious relationships with the world, others, and, most importantly, ourselves.

Since the sacral chakra is tied to the water element, it symbolizes ease and flow. When things like sensuality, feelings, and emotions are in question, the Svadhisthana empowers you to be freely expressive and flexible. So, when the chakra is balanced, fun and pleasure are paramount.

This chapter explores the physical, spiritual, and emotional symptoms commonly associated with a blocked sacral chakra. Understanding what a blocked Svadhisthana feels and looks like will help you identify whether you need to take corrective actions. Upon reading, you'll learn what causes the energy center to fall out of balance in the first place. Also included are some signs that it's activated and well-balanced. Finally, you'll come across a yoga sequence with step-by-step instructions. Incorporating it into your daily practice will help you activate your Svadhisthana and keep it balanced.

The Functions of the Svadhisthana

The Svadhisthana is associated with feelings of joy and pleasure. By extension, it is also connected to one's sensuality and sexuality. The sacral chakra plays a great role in supporting various aspects of a person's emotional and physical health. It is responsible for the bladder, sex organs, kidneys, and several body fluids.

The vital life energy remains dormant at the base of the spine until you activate it, thanks to various physical and spiritual activities. Now that you've balanced your root chakra, you're ready to extend the flow of the Kundalini energy further to balance your sacral chakra. When energy flows through this energy center, you can expect to feel as confident, stimulated, passionate, and spirited as ever. When balanced, you'll achieve better emotional health and heightened creativity and be more sensitive to your sensuality.

If you're struggling to maintain healthy relationships in your life, you can remedy this issue by working your sacral chakra. Balancing it will help you cultivate healthy boundaries, intimate connections, and better relationships.

As with any other chakra, experiencing a blockage in the Svadhisthana will deeply and negatively impact your mental, physical, and emotional health. Your overall well-being will be compromised. When the sacral chakra gets blocked, the five energy centers above it will fall out of balance.

What Causes a Blocked Sacral Chakra

A reluctance to change can contribute to a blockage in the sacral chakra. While this energy field encourages you to remain rational and collected, it also urges you to take action. This chakra favors acceptance, adaptation, flexibility, and freedom. If you feel stuck in the past or unable to accept certain life changes, it's always wise to do something about it.

The Svadhisthana rules over creativity and freedom of expression. It makes sense that this energy field will fall out of balance if you suppress your creativity. Likewise, repressing your passions, interests, and hobbies will obstruct energy flow through the sacral chakra. Whether you haven't had the time to practice what you're passionate about lately or find yourself in a situation where you must keep your hobbies and interests under the wraps, this can be quite detrimental to your mental and emotional health. Our sense of purpose is reignited when we do the things we love. If you don't have any current hobbies, think about all the things you wanted to do as a child but never got the chance to. This is your opportunity to heal your inner child. So, take the time to practice what you love to keep your sacral chakra in check, whether that's learning, playing sports, or crafting.

Lack of emotional unintelligence can also hinder energy flow through this chakra. Understanding and acknowledging your emotions without justifying them or judging yourself for them is necessary. Learning to identify everything you feel and knowing when to move away from negative emotions can help you improve your self-awareness and strengthen the Svadhisthana. Besides emotional intelligence, you must also listen to your body. We weren't put on this earth to sit at a desk for 7 hours a day, only to return home and plop down on the couch until it's bedtime. Being stuck in stagnant energy is a surefire way to block your sacral chakra as it creates tension in your lower back, hips, and, you guessed it, the sacral chakra. Move your body in any way that you like. You can get up and stretch every few hours, do some yoga, take a long morning or evening walk, or dance. It doesn't matter what you do as long as you get your body moving.

We are sane enough to realize we can't act on all our desires. Without self-discipline, boundaries would be overstepped, and safety would be compromised. However, this doesn't mean you shouldn't reward yourself every now and then. As long as you're not causing harm to yourself and others, allow yourself to give in to your wishes and desires from time to time. Suppressing pleasures is synonymous with the suppression of the Svadhisthana. Do you follow strict diet plans that make it impossible to enjoy food? Do you overwork yourself to the point of not having time for anything else? When was the last time you took a vacation or devised a travel plan and actually went through with it?

The Svadhisthana is associated with uniqueness and our sense of individuality. Each of us has a unique combination of experiences, skills, interests, and beliefs. Unfortunately, it's very easy to feel unremarkable in this increasingly competitive world. Overlooking your special attributes and individuality can obstruct your second energy center.

Did you know that the human body, particularly our cells and DNA, can store the energies and low vibrational frequencies that we acquire through difficult life experiences? If not healed, our vital life energy comes to a halt. While experiencing any trauma can negatively impact all your energy centers, sexual trauma is linked to a blocked sacral chakra. Resisting connection and intimacy also result in a weak Svadhisthana. This not only refers to sexual intimacy but isolating yourself from all intimate feelings and relationships also counts.

An Imbalanced Sacral Chakra

When your sacral chakra is blocked, you can expect to experience a wide range of mental, emotional, physical, and spiritual symptoms. These ailments correspond to the body parts and the emotional and behavioral qualities related to the Svadhisthana. An imbalanced sacral chakra will leave you feeling oddly weak and depressed. Experiencing a blockage in this center will make you excessively sensitive and anxious. When your energy flow is disturbed, you may struggle to overcome the paralyzing fear of losing control. This typically results in a series of obsessive-compulsive behaviors. The symptoms of this obstruction can be so overpowering to affect your professional and personal life.

Experiencing severe back pains is among the most common manifestations of an imbalanced sacral chakra. More serious physical conditions, like ovarian cysts, reproductive problems, lower-abdominal and pelvic issues, kidney and bladder problems, and urinary tract infections may also be triggered. Since the Sacral Chakra is associated with sensuality, issues like impotence and painful intercourse are not uncommon, either.

Having a blocked chakra can also affect how you think and how your mind works. People with a blocked sacral chakra tend to be codependent. They are also usually overtaken and deeply consumed by their emotions. A hindered flow of energy can cause you to either get lost in sexual fantasies or lose complete interest in sex. A blockage in that energy center is associated with a challenge in expressing creativity, needs, and feelings.

Physical Symptoms of a Blocked Sacral Chakra

- Arthritis
- Fatigue and lethargy
- Diminished energy levels
- Sexual and genital complications
- Kidney and spleen problems
- Joint conditions
- Hip problems
- Anemia
- Acute lower back pains
- Premenstrual syndrome

Mental Symptoms of a Blocked Sacral Chakra

- Diminished desire
- Detachment issues
- Decreased creativity
- Low libido
- Fear of experiencing pleasure
- Insecurity
- Excess sensitivity and emotional reactivity
- Codependency
- Addictive behaviors
- Anxiety
- Increased emotional attachments
- Aggressiveness

What a Balanced Sacral Chakra Feels Like

When your sacral chakra is balanced, you'll feel a deeper sense of love and self-care. To build healthy relationships with others and the world around you, having a secure connection with yourself is imperative. This is what the sacral chakra is responsible for. When it's activated, your understanding of the need for self-care and compassion will grow with each passing day. You'll learn to put yourself first and create boundaries that will help you safeguard your energy.

A balanced Svadhisthana also compels you to reflect on your relationships with others. When you realize your self-worth, you better understand the things you want and expect in all your connections. You'll inevitably re-evaluate your professional, familial, and romantic relationships and let go of those that no longer serve you. At the same time, you'll strengthen your healthy relationships and foster connections that bring intimacy, pleasure, and joy.

With energy flowing freely in the sacral chakra, you'll feel an increased sense of vitality and inspiration. Your creative powers will be reinvigorated, which will ultimately help you manifest positive life experiences. You'll also better understand how you can best express yourself, creatively speaking.

An activated sacral chakra will make you feel in tune and aligned with your physical body. You'll grow more comfortable in your being and prioritize nourishing it, ensuring its overall well-being. Realizing what gives you pleasure and how you can use your body to partake in joyful life experiences will be triggered.

A healthy Svadhisthana makes it easier to adapt and accept change. It also promotes a better understanding of life cycles, which increases your consciousness and awareness. This is something you can use to manifest the life you desire. There will never be a dull moment when this energy center is at its optimum function. Everything that you do will bring along a sense of excitement. You'll also no longer feel the need to resist your desires and feel more confident in doing things that bring you joy and happiness.

When your sacral chakra is balanced, you become more aware of your subconscious beliefs. As we've seen, the root chakra is all about one's survival needs. The Svadhisthana, on the other hand, is concerned with desire and pleasure. Embracing your creative energies will make you aware of the beliefs you have accepted as your own. This way, you'll be able to identify the thoughts that hold you back and the authentic views that you may have suppressed due to societal pressure.

Yoga Sequence for the Svadhisthana

Incorporating asanas and yoga into your daily practice can help alleviate numerous aspects of your life. Certain yoga poses focus on specific chakras and parts of the body. Practicing them can help you release tension in those areas and boost your vibrational energy. The following yoga sequence will help you balance your sacral chakra and keep it active:

Utkata Konasana - Goddess Pose

Goddess pose.

1. Stand up straight with both feet wide apart. Your toes should point outward. Bend your knees generously so your thighs are parallel to the floor. You may not be able to get this right the first time around, which is fine.
2. Your knees should align with the middle of your feet, and your shoulders should be kept right above your hips.
3. Extend the crown of your head toward the sky and focus on keeping your tailbone pointed downward.
4. Bring both palms together, parallel to the heart.
5. Stay in this position for 8 to 10 deep breaths.

Viparita Virabhadrasana - Reverse Warrior Pose

Reverse warrior pose.

1. From the Utkata Konasana pose, move your back heel outward, turning your hips rightward as you do so. Your heel should be flat on the mat, and your toes somewhat turned.
2. Your balance may feel off at first. If you can't maintain the pose, you can move your right foot outward closer to the edge of the mat.
3. Place your hands in front of you, extending them at shoulders level. Move your right palm upward as you arch upward and back to your normal position. Calmly slide your left hand, placing it along the length of the leg at the back.
4. Focus on maintaining the strength in your legs as you relax your upper body.
5. Stay in this pose for around 4 breaths, then repeat on the other side.

Prasarita Padottanasana C - Wide-Legged Forward Bend C

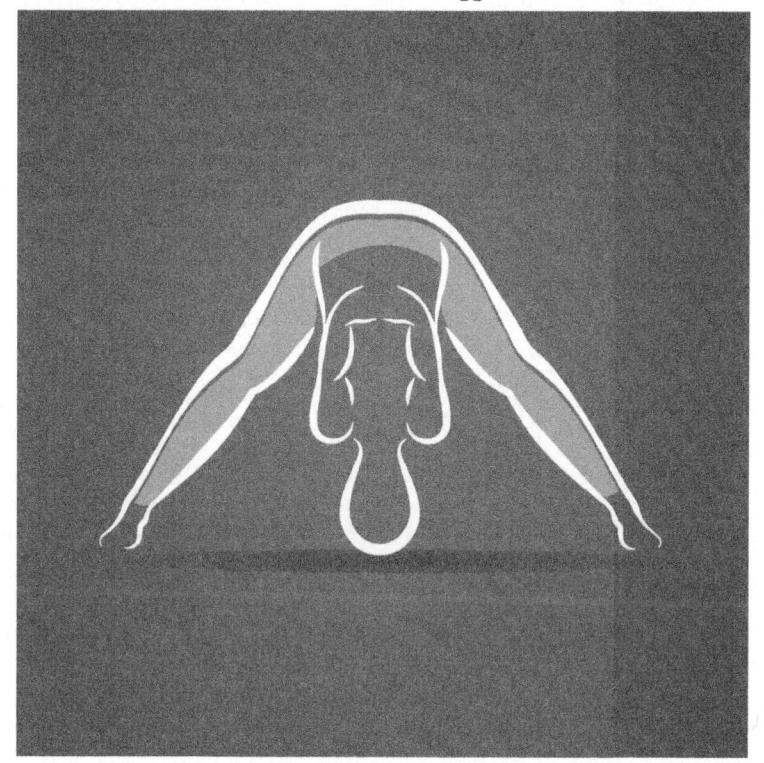

Wide-legged forward bend C.

1. Return to the initial stance. Stand up straight with both feet wide apart and your toes pointing forward.
2. Take your arms behind your back and interlace your fingers. Rest them on the bone at the base of your spine (known as the sacrum).
3. Push your shoulders back and keep your shoulder blades down, extending your arms downward in the process.
4. Hinge your hips forward, folding your upper body so the crown of your head points towards the floor.
5. Shift your weight so your hips are aligned with your heels. Resist the feeling that you may stumble and trust your body.
6. Stay in this pose for 5 to 10 breaths. To unfold yourself from the pose, lengthen the crown of your head and carefully pull yourself up.

Paschimottanasana - Seated Forward Bend

Seated forward bend.

1. Bring yourself to a seated position and extend your legs in front of you. Press your heels into the mat and keep your feet flexed. Try to soften your toes.
2. Inhale as you bring your hands over your head with your palms facing each other. As you exhale, move your arms forward, and reach down for your feet. When moving your upper body, lead with your heart instead of bending down with your lower back.
3. Keep your back and torso flexed as you do so.
4. Feel the stretch at the base of your spine as you stay in this pose for at least 14 slow and steady breaths.

Supta Baddha Konasana - Reclined Bound Angle Pose

Reclined bound angle pose.

1. Lie down on your back and bend your knees outward. Allow the soles of your feet to touch each other, letting your knees drop towards the floor. You can place blocks beneath each knee for extra support if you're not flexible.
2. Allow your palms to rest on your belly with your elbows resting on the ground.
3. Inhale normally, but allow your body to get heavier with each exhale.
4. Focus on widening the space in your hips and pelvic area. Practice makes perfect.
5. Reflect on your creative power and draw affirmations on how you believe in your abilities.
6. Stay in this pose for as long as needed.

In your journey to balancing this energy center, you'll feel prompted to work on all the relationships in your life. You'll also realize that your creative power has no boundaries. As you work with the Svadhisthana, you'll better understand how you can build a healthy, sustainable relationship with pleasure. The healing journey serves as a great eye-opener, as it will allow you to unlock your deepest emotions and recognize the way you react to various things. You'll learn to sit comfortably with the intensity of your emotions. This level of enlightenment, self-awareness, and inner peace will allow you to achieve a higher level of self-expression regarding your feelings, wants, and needs. Ultimately, you'll gain great insight into how to express yourself effectively and clearly and set healthy boundaries in all your relationships.

Chapter 5: Balance Your Solar Plexus Chakra

Located above your navel, the solar plexus chakra is the third center in your chakra system. Physically, it rules over your abdominal area and unites and controls energy sources from digestive organs such as the stomach, upper intestines, liver, pancreas, and gallbladder. This center is linked to vitality, self-actualization, and self-confidence on the emotional and spiritual front. It's also called *Manipura*, which is the conjunction of the Sanskrit words: *mani*, which means "gem," and *pura*, which means "city." Manipura can be translated as the city of jewels, referring to the chakra being a person's emotional, mental, and physical treasure center.

To imagine the center of your spiritual development, the best way to visualize a yellow orb of light just above your navel – exactly how Manipura is described. Due to its association with the fire element and the Sun, the solar plexus chakra is often represented by the colors yellow and gold. Like these two elements of nature, Manipura represents a continuous supply of energy necessary to maintain your overall well-being.

From this chapter, you'll learn how the healthy function of Manipura affects your health and happiness and how you may feel when this chakra is out of balance. You'll be provided with a simple yoga sequence designed to balance your solar plexus chakra, so you can relieve the symptoms of blockage you may experience. Since opening this chakra is a rather intense experience, you'll also be cautioned about the symptoms that may arise when Manipura starts to realign.

The Functions of Manipura

Given its location in the body, the functions of the solar plexus chakra are mainly tied to self-confidence, purpose, inner power, and self-esteem. This is because your energy lies at the base of your spine and travels upwards to Manipura whenever needed. Here, it activates the centers for self-expression (often referred to as gut instincts) while reassuring you about how you choose to express yourself. This keeps you motivated to establish more goals and take a proactive approach to reach them. In turn, your goals aid you in finding and fulfilling your life's purpose.

The solar plexus chakra has many functions, chief of which include:

- **Providing Identity:** The energy of Manipura fuels the core of your personality, making it possible to express your authentic self and withstand social pressures.

- **Developing Your Instincts:** Staying true to yourself hinges on your ability to tap into your instincts. The solar plexus chakra keeps your instincts sharp and present.

- **Source of Personal Power:** It provides you with the strength needed to rein in your emotions, focus your thoughts, and take action towards improving your life.

- **Giving Intention to Your Actions:** To achieve the life goals you have set for yourself, you will need the help of this chakra to channel your thoughts into forming an intention.

- **Instilling Self-Confidence:** Manipura affects how you view yourself, mentally and physically. By providing you with a clear picture of your skills, it's making you more self-assured.

- **Maintaining Digestive Health:** This chakra acts as a digestive aid and helps prevent conditions like muscle hernias, ulcers, gallbladder stones, or diabetes.

What Causes a Blocked Solar Plexus Chakra

Since the solar plexus chakra affects the most vulnerable parts of ourselves (our intuition and self-confidence), it doesn't take much to shake it out of balance. On some occasions, the causes of this chakra being blocked are inactive, overactive, or physical. These typically stem from conditions originating in other organs or organ systems that will move on to feed on the energy in your solar plexus if left untreated. After all, these systems are under the control of the other chakras, and they are all interconnected. What affects one will ultimately affect the others, too.

In most cases, the causes of your third chakra being blocked are mental or emotional. One of the biggest culprits lies in unhealthy social connections. In today's society, it's not uncommon to face unrealistic expectations, even from your loved ones. And when facing the pressure that comes from such sources, you are more than tempted to give in, causing you to lose sight of what you want. Your instinct tries to warn you against this, but the more the burden grows on your solar plexus, the more your ability to listen to your gut diminishes.

Experiencing a traumatic or dangerous situation is another common cause of unfounded fears and the feeling of helplessness associated with the third chakra. Trauma stemming from rejection or the invalidation of your opinion can also lead to issues with Manipura. These types of interactions can result in both an inactive and overactive center. You may either become less than confident and give in to the will of others in fear of another rejection. Or, you put on a seeming bold front, become critical and controlling even over the actions of others and start taking hazardous risks.

Signs of an Imbalanced or Blocked Manipura

A blocked, inactive, or overactive solar plexus chakra can induce a broad range of symptoms. Due to the physical location of the chakra, most symptoms manifest as physical disturbances in the abdominal area (including the back part). However, the mental consequences of Manipura's malfunction are much more extensive and overwhelming.

In fact, the first signs of a blocked solar plexus chakra are typically mental ones. The path of energy in Manipura is often blocked due to several stressors, and it happens gradually over an extended period, without you noticing it. It may all begin with the loss of self-confidence, which restrains you from expressing your emotions and realizing plans. You soon start experiencing physical symptoms as well, and it will look like everything that can go wrong in your life does go wrong. As you feel the control slipping from your hands, in a desperate attempt to take it back, you reach for emotional and mental tools that only make things worse. Below is a quick summary of the physical and mental symptoms that may indicate a blocked third chakra.

Physical Symptoms of a Blocked Solar Plexus Chakra

- Gastrointestinal issues
- Gallbladder issues
- Pancreas malfunctions, including diabetes
- Lack of energy
- Pulling muscles easily
- Lower respiratory issues

Mental Symptoms of a Blocked Solar Plexus Chakra

- Exaggerated fear of rejection
- Disproportionate aggression
- Insecurity and indecisiveness
- Low self-esteem levels
- Frequent negative thoughts
- Helplessness and lack of purpose
- Desire to control and criticize

- Being overly judgmental

What the Opening of the Solar Plexus Chakra Feels Like

Unlike in some other chakras, where the first signs of their opening arrive almost unnoticed, you will undoubtedly sense when energy starts to flow through Manipura. The sudden burst of energy is often painful and is accompanied by one or more of the following symptoms:

- **Lack of Sleep:** You may start experiencing sleepless nights and continue tossing and turning soon after you have begun engaging Manipura. When it opens, you'll sleep even better than you did before.

- **Loss of Appetite:** As you start engaging your core muscles and twist and turn your internal organs, they may slow their functions first, leaving you without appetite. It will return once your metabolism gets over the initial stress and kicks into a higher gear.

- **Tremors and Palpitations:** The release of pent-up energy combined with the activation of muscles can cause you to experience small tremors throughout your body. Likewise, palpitations are caused by the shaking of heart muscles.

- **Light-Headedness:** The tremors will leave your muscles and nerves temporarily depleted of energy, causing you to feel lightheaded. Cease what you were doing for a few minutes, and your energy will soon return with a vengeance.

- **Fluctuating Energy Levels:** The burst of energy may not last too long. One day you'll be so energized that you feel you can take on the world, and the next won't even feel like getting up from the bed. This fluctuation lasts for a long time.

- **Nausea:** This is another symptom of your internal organs being overworked. It can be contained by drinking lots of water and will pass after deep breathing exercises.

- **Emotional Instability:** Your emotions can also fluctuate drastically. On some days, you can have a confident, positive outlook on life. On others, you'll return to being the pessimistic and critical person you were before you started opening Manipura.

Typically, as soon as Manipura opens, all these symptoms disappear. When your solar plexus chakra is fully open and balanced, you feel in control and confident in your abilities. You can exercise enough self-discipline to take responsibility for your life instead of blaming and criticizing others for everything that's happening to you. You'll also gain the ability to make rational decisions and devise well-thought-out plans. All this will help you overcome your fears and adopt an independent lifestyle.

If any of the issues persist, this may point to another energy center being blocked. It's a good idea to look into them so you can open them and free your entire spiritual-energetic system.

Yoga Sequences for the Manipura

When out of balance, the third chakra creates a significant energy imbalance, making it harder to restore the natural flow to this center. The following yoga sequence will help you regain your inner strength and confidence. It contains several yoga poses, mudras, mantras, and even a powerful deep breathing technique.

Virabhadra III

Virabhadra III.

Also called the third Warrior pose, Virabhadra III is an excellent start for building your confidence. It helps you get in the mood for an empowering yoga session. Here's how to do it:

1. Start in a standing position, and shift your balance onto one of your legs.
2. Move the other leg backward and your arms forward until your body is parallel to the ground.
3. When you feel that your weight has been transferred from your leg to your core, repeat the mantra "I can because I am strong."
4. Use your breathing to support you while holding the pose for a few more seconds.

Parsvottanasana

Pyramid pose

Parsvottanasana, or the Pyramid pose, is also designed to strengthen your core and mental resolve. This will prepare you for the more demanding exercises in this sequence. Here is how to perform it:

1. Place your right foot about 3-4 feet in front of your body.
2. Place your hands on your sacral area to check your hips are at an even height.
3. Move your hand behind your back into a prayer position.
4. Fold your body over your right leg until your stomach touches your knee.

5. Activate your core by elevating your knees. This will cause the balance to shift from your foot to your thighs and then to your abdominal muscles.

Navasana

Navasana.

Kennguru, CC BY 3.0 <https://creativecommons.org/licenses/by/3.0>, via Wikimedia Commons: https://commons.wikimedia.org/wiki/File:Paripurna-Navasana_Yoga-Asana_Nina-Mel.jpg

Navasana, or Boat pose, is the first intense exercise in this sequence. By lowering your body to the ground, this pose connects your abdominal area with the earth, empowering you through it. Here is how to do Navasana:

1. Sit on a mat with your legs in front of you and your shoulders rolled back.
2. Lean back until you feel that your core can keep you upright. Your balance should be on your sitting bones.
3. Inhale and start bringing your legs closer by lifting them off the mat until only your toes are touching it.
4. Lift your legs all the way up in front of you. Hold them just below your knee on the inside of your thighs to maintain your balance.
5. Remove your hand from your legs and extend them in the air on either side of your knees. Keep your hands parallel to your legs for at least five seconds.

Purvottanasana

Reverse plank pose.

Also called the Reverse Plank pose, Purvottanasana activates your core so it can help you raise yourself whenever you need it. Here is how to do this pose:

1. Sit in an upright position and bend your knees, bringing them slightly closer to your body.
2. Place your knees hip distance apart and slowly lower your elbows onto the mat behind you.
3. Move one palm behind your back where your elbow was resting naturally in the previous step, then repeat with the other palm.
4. Take a deep breath, and by engaging your core muscles, lift your hips up towards the ceiling. This will ground you at the back of your heels and the base of your fingers.
5. Let your head fall back naturally and hold the position for five to ten breaths.

Surya Mudra

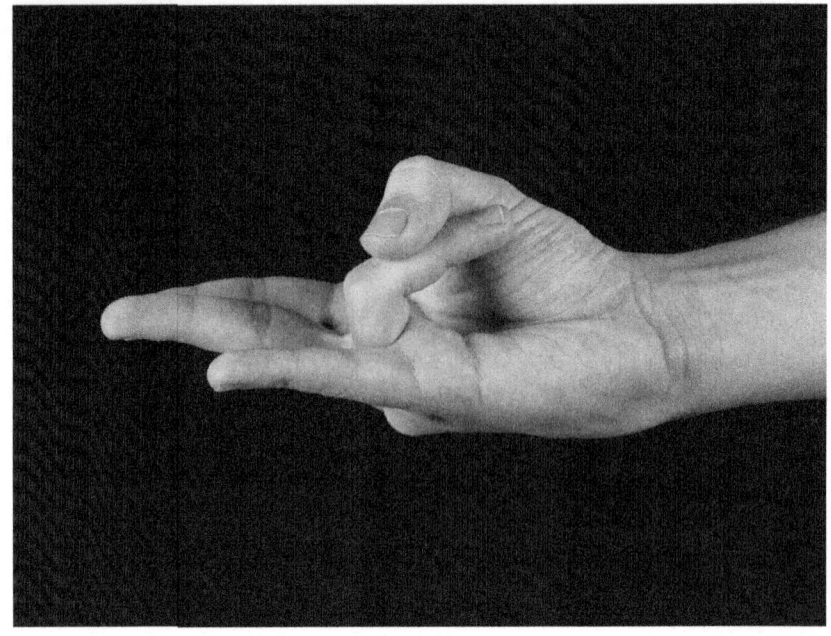

Surya Mudra.

The previous yoga pose was rather demanding for your core. To counteract it, the Sun Mudra (or Surya Mudra) will reinforce your mental resolve to engage your body and mind continually in the following poses. Here is how to perform this mudra:

1. Start in a seated position with your hands resting on your legs slightly in front of you.
2. Bend your ring fingers towards your palms and place your thumbs over them.
3. Hold this hand position for five minutes while breathing in and out deeply to enhance the vitality of your body and mind.

Ardha Matsyendrasana

Half Lord of the Fishes pose.

Ardha Matsyendrasana (or the Half Lord of the Fishes pose) engages your spinal column, which adds another layer to the activation of your core and Manipura. Here are the steps for this pose:

1. Sit in an upright position, and bring your knees close to your body.
2. Bend your right knee sideways and cross the left one over it.
3. By pressing your inner thigh towards your abdomen, bring your left knee to an upright position.
4. Place your right arm over your left knee and your left arm behind your back.
5. Rotate your back as much as your spine allows it, and you can still remain grounded on your sitting bones.
6. To fully engage your spine and let the energy through it and into Manipura, twist your neck while holding the pose for five breaths.

Savasana

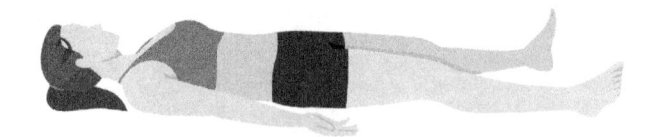

Corpse pose.

Corpse pose, or Savasana, is the most effective for your solar plexus chakra when combined with deep breathing techniques. The following steps will show you how to do it:

1. Lie on the mat with your back flat and your hands extended beside your body.
2. Move your hands away from your body, palms up, while still keeping them on the ground.
3. Inhale deeply through your nose, and feel the air traveling through your body.
4. Pause when you feel your body is filled with air until your diaphragm can't expand anymore, and exhale through your nose.
5. Repeat until you feel your heart slowing down and your body and mind are enveloped in a deep state of relaxation.

Dhanurasana

Bow pose.)

The previous pose transitions well into the Dhanurasana, or Bow pose. This one is designed to complete the Manipura and rebalance this energy center by opening the dorsal ends of your abdominal muscles. Here is how to do this pose:

1. Turn over to your stomach and bend your knees upwards.
2. Place your hands on the outer portion of your ankles to keep them firmly in place.
3. Take a deep breath and lift your upper body and thighs as much as your spine allows you to.
4. Maintain your weight on your lower abdomen for five breaths while lifting your head and looking in front of you.

As you can see, this sequence of poses focuses on strengthening your abdominal muscles, which play a fundamental role in activating Manipura. It also enhances the flexibility of your spine in the same area, grounding your entire body and allowing the energy to radiate through it. Combined with deep breathing exercises, mudras, and mantras, this sequence will help you relax and reconnect with your intuition. Feel free to add any affirmations or spiritual aids you feel necessary to overcome personal concerns or unhealthy tendencies to compare yourself to others. You have all the energy you need for this inside your chakra system. All you need is to find the way to free its path toward Manipura.

While most poses should be maintained for at least five breaths or seconds, if you have a severe blockage, your physical symptoms may not allow this in the beginning. If you have any difficulties holding them this long, feel free to do it until it feels comfortable. As your energy levels improve, so will your ability to maintain the poses. Apart from these empowering yoga poses, you may also help restore balance to your solar plexus by engaging in a healthier lifestyle. This includes a balanced diet, more exercise, or even walking in nature and letting sunlight reinvigorate your body.

An alternative would be to perform restorative yoga poses before a fireplace or any other open fire source. The more Manipura healing exercises you can implement into your life, the sooner you'll open or unblock your solar plexus chakra. A healthier lifestyle will provide you with more energy to complete your exercises and enhance your ability to focus on your intention of opening or balancing the third chakra. This will allow you to return to your confident and relaxed self, and you'll finally feel in complete control over your life.

Chapter 6: Heal Your Heart Chakra

Also called Anahata, the heart chakra is the fourth of the seven chakras. As the name indicates, it is located in the middle of the spine, at the level of the heart. Anahata is a Sanskrit word that means unhurt, unbeaten, and unstruck. The heart chakra is where your deepest truth lies, the feelings you struggle to put into words. The element of this chakra is air, which is quite fitting. Like love, the air is everywhere around us and inside us, and we can feel it even with our eyes closed. When the heart chakra is open, your energy can resemble the air flowing freely inside of you. Green is the heart chakra's color and is associated with the energy of love and transformation. The symbol of the Anahata is a six-pointed green star in a flower with 12 petals, and its mantra is "I love."

Close your eyes now. Try to assess what you are feeling at this very moment. Are you scared? Are you anxious? Do you feel loved? Do you feel joyful? If you find yourself more consumed with negative feelings, your Anahata may be blocked and in need of healing. Love, hatred, and fear aren't often experienced simultaneously. One of these emotions usually takes over while the other two stay in the background. You may still experience these emotions even when in the background, but they aren't as strong as those in control. For instance, fear and hatred can be in the background when you are in love. However, after a heartbreak or a painful breakup, fear or hatred becomes the predominant emotion, while love takes the backseat until you heal and are ready to open your heart once again.

The heart chakra doesn't develop at a very young age and usually starts when a person begins exploring more mature relationships. It commonly develops somewhere between the ages of 21 and 28. This is when many people experience real and true love for the first time and have the courage to put themselves out there, at the risk of facing heartbreak or rejection.

Numerous things in our day-to-day lives can impact the heart chakra. For this reason, you must pay attention to it and make sure it is always open. A balanced heart chakra will enable you to experience various positive feelings like happens, joy, and unconditional love, which can help you enjoy life in newer and better ways.

An open heart chakra brings many positive emotions like self-love, joy, and trust, while a closed one can make you spiteful, untrusting, or pessimistic. As we know, emotions have a tremendous impact on our physical health and mental well-being. When emotions aren't managed, you'll feel stressed, worried, and even depressed. These negative emotions can siphon off positive feelings like love and joy. This is when your heart chakra will require healing.

Did you know the Earth had its own heart chakra as well? In Southwestern England, between Shaftesbury and Glastonbury, lies the planet's own Anahata. Just a few miles away, the enchanting and mystic Stonehenge monument makes this area even more fascinating.

The Functions of the Heart Chakra

Due to its unique position as the fourth chakra, the Anahata can be considered the halfway point of the seven chakras. It acts as a bridge between the upper and lower chakras to unify their spiritual and physical aspects. The Anahata is the center of our feelings and emotions, including joy, empathy, forgiveness, compassion, self-love, and how we feel towards other people. The Anahata rules over your sense of gratitude, peace, generosity, trust, transformation, change, deep relationships, and emotional control.

A balanced heart chakra helps you achieve self-acceptance and creates harmony between you and the world. When the prana is awakened, and the heart energy flows through the Anahata, a person begins to experience feelings like self-love, happiness, and high self-esteem. As a result, you feel motivated, inspired, and aware of your purpose in life.

What Causes a Blocked Anahata

Various things can be responsible for blocking the Anahata. You need to dig deep within yourself to discover the factors that have caused the imbalance in your heart chakra. Since it is associated with feelings like love and joy, the Anahata can be blocked by experiencing opposite feelings like hatred or sadness.

An Imbalanced Heart Chakra

Feelings of unconditional love stem from the heart chakra. When open, you feel this love flowing through every part of your being. You feel open and ready to give and receive love. Now, when the heart chakra is imbalanced, you experience feelings of hatred, fear, and hurt. Some people say the opposite of love is hate, but it can also be fear. So, when your heart chakra is blocked, you start to experience a tightness in your chest and an inauspicious feeling.

Of those who have experienced trauma in their lives, some were able to move on, whereas others are still haunted by their past. If you feel you cannot let go of the past, your heart chakra may be blocked. You are unable to forgive and learn to love yourself once again.

It is normal to reminisce about a previous relationship and feel nostalgic (or relieved if it was a bad relationship). However, if you find yourself unable to move on from a past relationship that you know wouldn't have worked, this is another sign your heart chakra is blocked. You are still thinking about your ex-partner and obsessing over your relationship instead of processing why it didn't work out and why you need to move on.

Low self-esteem is another sign of a blockage in your heart chakra. The Anahata is the center of self-love, so your heart chakra requires serious attention if you are prone to low self-esteem and self-doubt. Lack of self-love can also make you neglect your own needs. You begin putting others first and forget to take care of yourself. For this reason, you may need to set healthy boundaries to protect yourself and regain your assurance.

Holding grudges is another symptom you need to look out for. Grudges consume you with negativity and can even ruin your relationships, especially if the person feels guilty and has already apologized. Opening the heart chakra can pave the way to forgiveness and help you let go. If you shut yourself off from the people in your life and push them away, your heart chakra becomes imbalanced. You may think you are protecting yourself from being hurt, but no one can live without being surrounded by people. As a result, you'll end up feeling lonely and depressed.

While occasionally experiencing stress is normal, a blockage in your heart chakra can leave you unable to handle the stress or anxiety in your life. In time, these factors can cause mental and physical health issues. Suppressing emotions is another sign your heart chakra needs healing. In fact, it isn't healthy to keep your emotions bottled up since they can erupt as anger outbursts, or you may resort to unhealthy coping habits, like drinking or substance abuse. This can have serious consequences on your relationships, not to mention your mental health at large. Remember, there are always healthy ways to express your emotions without hurting others' feelings.

Those with a balanced chakra are trusting and don't go around doubting everyone in their lives (that isn't to say they are gullible; they just know who to trust). So, when your heart chakra is blocked, all your old emotional baggage starts to sneak into your life, plaguing you with trust issues. This will prevent you from developing healthy relationships and may even cost you those you have.

If you have empathy, your root chakra is well-balanced, but when you cannot put yourself in someone's shoes or show compassion, you must work on opening the heart chakra. By contrast, being overly empathetic is a symptom of a blocked chakra since, as mentioned, it will make you prioritize others and neglect yourself.

Many of these feelings are quite normal, and we occasionally feel them. However, if you experience them for a prolonged period of time, chances are your heart chakra is blocked and requires tending to.

Physical Symptoms of a Blocked Heart Chakra

A blocked heart chakra can manifest itself through various physical symptoms, including:

- Weak immune system
- Issues with the heart, lungs, breast, and thymus
- Asthma
- Insomnia
- Tightness in areas around the heart (chest, shoulders, and arms)
- Upper back pain
- Blood circulation issues
- Early signs of aging

Mental Symptoms of a Blocked Heart Chakra

You will also experience one or more of these mental symptoms:

- Anxiety
- Depression
- Shyness
- Lack of empathy
- Inability to forgive
- Loneliness
- Commitment issues
- Playing the victim

What a Balanced Heart Chakra Feels Like

Once your heart chakra opens, you'll begin to feel its impact on all areas of your life, starting with your emotional and mental health.

One of the first and most powerful feelings you'll experience is gratitude. You'll start to appreciate what you have and be open to receiving what you desire.

In parallel, you'll also begin to experience feelings of forgiveness and compassion towards others and yourself. You'll show empathy and understanding, which will make it easier for you to forgive and forget, let go of past hurts, and open yourself to new experiences. Instead of dwelling over your past mistakes, you'll use the lessons you have learned to cultivate better and healthier relationships. You'll become more relaxed and won't experience the same levels of anxiety you did before. When your heart chakra is awakened, you begin feeling, experiencing, and living everything from the heart, at the moment, without any regrets or concerns about the future. This will reduce your worries and stress and allow you to be more at peace.

You start consciously developing healthy relationships as you open your heart and unshackle yourself from the past. You'll make better choices when it comes to romantic involvement instead of toxic ones that only drain your time and energy. You'll experience self-love and acceptance, which will motivate you to stay away from the people who don't add value to your life and move toward those who lift you up and help you grow. You'll become your truest self around your loved ones and offer them unconditional love.

Once you begin to experience emotions on a deeper level, know that your heart chakra is beginning to open. Since the Anahata is the center of unconditional love, you'll experience emotions related to this feeling like joy, happiness, belonging, and optimism. You'll enjoy the little things in life that you may have taken for granted before, like a majestic sunset or a nice cup of morning coffee.

The sensation of tightness you may have once felt in your chest will give way to a pleasant and soothing lightness. It will feel like the world's weight was on your shoulders, and now it is gone. You'll learn to trust again after having had your guard up for so long. You won't only have faith in others *but in yourself.* You'll be able to fiercely believe in your ability to handle whatever life throws at you.

The Anahata awakening won't happen all at once but rather in stages. You'll experience strong and overpowering emotions during the first stages as you realize you deserve a better, more gratifying life. At that point, you'll experience intense crying. As you keep practicing various methods to open your heart chakra, you should be ready for its awakening at any time. The chakra will open suddenly, and you'll begin approaching life from a newer, more positive viewpoint.

However, recovery is a complex journey, and there will be days when you'll revert to your old self. Don't fret or feel bad; this is normal. You'll experience ups and downs until you reach your destination. Once the Anahata is fully opened, your consciousness will shift. Naturally, you'll still face challenges, stress, anxiety, and setbacks, but with an open chakra, handling and overcoming these challenges won't prove as daunting as they once did.

Yoga Sequence for the Heart Chakra

What follows is a yoga sequence to help open your heart chakra. Before practicing, we recommend you repeat this powerful mantra: I will live with an open heart. Focus on your breathing and let the mantra motivate you while practicing.

Anjaneyasana - Low Lunge

Low lunge.

This pose will help you find balance when facing an unpleasant situation. It also encourages you to step out of your comfort zone.

1. First, take the Adho Mukha Svanasana pose (downward facing dog), then step your right foot forward between your hands. This will align your right knee over your heel.
2. Next, lower your left knee to the floor without moving your right knee.
3. Now, slide your left knee back until you begin to feel a stretch in the front of your left thigh.
4. Draw your tailbone in the direction of the floor, then lift your pubic bone towards your navel.
5. Gradually, lift your arms and chest upwards to frame your head.
6. Relax your shoulders while drawing the blades on your back.
7. Lift your gaze and practice five rounds of breath, then switch to the other side

Salamba Bhujangasana - Sphinx Pose

Sphinx pose.

This pose is a gentle opener that stimulates your heart chakra and awakens it.

1. Lie down on your stomach.
2. Place your elbows underneath your shoulders.
3. Relax your shoulders. As your shoulder blades slide down your back, you will feel a slight lift in your chest.

4. Focus your breathing on your abdomen and lower back.
5. Bring both elbows to your sides, place your palms on top of one another, and gently place your forehead over your hands to finish the pose.

Natarajasana - Dancer's Pose

Dancer's pose.

This pose keeps you stable, at ease, and peaceful.

1. Take the Tadasana (mountain) pose.
2. Breathe in and place your weight on your right foot. Press the top of your right thigh back into your hip joint.
3. Pull your knee up so your standing leg remains strong and straight.
4. Next, lift your left foot off the mat and move it towards your left glute.
5. Using your left hand, hold the inside of your foot.
6. Stretch your right arm to be aligned with your ear.
7. Gently press your foot into your left hand and lean your torso forward.
8. Stretch your right arm forward to be in front of your torso.
9. Remain in this pose for about 20-30 seconds.
10. Release by letting go of your foot and placing it on the floor.
11. Repeat the same steps with your other foot.

Urdhva Mukha Shvanasana - Upward-Facing Dog Pose

Upward facing dog pose

This pose will strengthen your arms and promote flexibility in your spine.

1. Lie down on your mat, making sure your feet lay flat on the mat as well.
2. Place your palms under your shoulders and allow your shoulders to point upwards.
3. Lift your head, shoulders, and neck off the matt by pressing your hands.
4. Lift your quads off the mat by pressing into the tops of your feet.
5. Gaze forward to keep your neck neutral and support.

Virabhadrasana - Warrior I Pose

Warrior I pose.

This pose includes a gentle backbend to help unblock the Anahata energy.

1. Take the warrior I pose by standing with your front knee stacked over your front ankle.
2. Plant your back foot firmly on the ground at a 90° angle.
3. Place your hands on your lower back and gradually move them down to your back leg.
4. Move your hips forward and lift your chest up.

Setu Bandha Sarvangasana - Bridge Pose

Bridge pose.

This pose strengthens the spine and opens your Anahata towards the sky.

1. Lie down on your back with your feet on the mat and your knees pointing upwards.
2. Place your arms by your sides and your palms facing downwards by your hips.
3. Breathe in and press into your feet to lift your hips upwards.
4. Distribute your weight between your feet and your shoulders' base. Try not to put pressure on your head and neck.
5. To come out of this pose, gently lower your spine while exhaling.

Ultimately, opening your heart chakra will tremendously benefit various aspects of your life, from your self-love and confidence to your relationships. Take a few minutes each day to practice these yoga sequences, and you'll begin to feel a difference. It will take time and effort, so be patient with yourself and stay consistent.

Chapter 7: Clear Your Throat Chakra

As the fifth chakra in your energetic system, the throat chakra plays a fundamental role in keeping you mentally and physically healthy. This chakra is also known as Vishuddha, the Sanskrit term for the phrase "extremely pure." Its name and association with the color blue indicate a clear connection between this chakra and the purity of the air element. Given its location, Vishuddha is often described as a transparent blue or white pocket of air sitting at the back of your throat, near the wall of your neck muscles and spine.

When blocked, the throat chakra emits small yet indicative signals that something is wrong in your body, signs that should never be ignored. Of course, this doesn't mean you should panic when you notice them. It simply means it's time for you to address them before they cause more harm.

From this chapter, you'll learn how a balanced function of Vishuddha affects your health and happiness and how you may feel when this chakra is out of balance. You'll be provided with a simple yoga sequence designed to clear your throat chakra and alleviate the symptoms of the fallout you may experience from the blockage of this energy center. The opening of this chakra is subtler than with other chakras, so you'll also be provided with the symptoms you can expect when the energy starts to flow through.

The Functions of Vishuddha

Vishuddha plays a key role in your energetic system. It's responsible for providing you with communication skills, both internally and verbally. The throat chakra helps align your thoughts and heart with your speech so you can voice whatever lies inside them in a more balanced way. It also gives you a creative outlet for those emotions and ideas you simply can't express through genuine conversations. Since your creative notions come from your sacral chakra, it means your ability to express yourself is conditioned by the health of this lower energetic center. It also indicates that one of the crucial functions of Vishuddha is to work together with other chakras.

Creativity teaches you to accept your experiences and embrace your unique talents. Seeing how many skills you possess often helps you realize that others also have their own original ideas and talents. The energy flowing through Vishuddha compels you to pay more attention to those around you, allowing you to develop healthier relationships.

Awakening your life's energy and letting it flow through your throat chakra freely through yoga and mindfulness practices affects its physical functions. The heightened ability to self-express clears your mind, chasing away your worries. This results in better sleep quality, more energy for your daily tasks, and a healthier body overall.

Your throat chakra rules over organs with critical roles in your body. One of these is the thyroid, the endocrine gland responsible for growth, immunity, cognitive functions, the work of other endocrine organs, and much more. Your respiratory tract also falls under Vishuddha's responsibilities. So do your neck and mouth area with all the muscles, blood vessels, and other tissue inherently capable of absorbing energy.

What Causes a Blocked Throat Chakra

There could be many reasons for your throat chakra being blocked. Generally, the most common ones stem from the lower chakra. Natural lifeforce enters your body at your root chakra, and since all chakras are interconnected, the energy must travel towards the upper centers. Now, if the lower chakras are blocked, they won't let the energy flow towards the throat chakra, throwing it out of balance. Likewise, if they are overactive, they will send a boost of energy your throat chakra can't handle, causing it to get overworked.

Physical conditions, such as upper respiratory infections and hyper or hypothyroidism, can be both the causes and symptoms of a Vishuddha malfunction. These conditions often appear secondary to other physical issues, so they are often mistaken for those. If left untreated for too long, they will start affecting the throat center on a physical, mental, and emotional pain.

Emotional and mental issues also play an enormous role in blocking the throat chakra, originating from multiple sources. Physical trauma can lead to a mental one and hinder you from expressing your pain and other negative emotions. Emotional trauma can also develop independently from a physical one. For instance, you can suffer an emotional trauma you feel too embarrassed to talk about. Hiding your pain will make you feel anxious or depressed, which can be detrimental to your immune system and can lead to a wide range of physical symptoms.

If you were forced to keep your desires and true to yourself for a long time, your throat chakra may go inactive out of inertia, even if the energy would normally flow through it. This pattern can often be seen in verbal and emotional abuse or gaslighting victims.

Signs of an Imbalanced or Blocked Vishuddha

As mentioned earlier, the signs of your throat chakra malfunctioning are often very subtle. It may start by not being able to express a particular emotion and slowly progress to preventing you from speaking freely in social settings. Instead of expressing your thoughts and feelings, you may start inventing others that you know would please the people you are conversing with.

If the balance in this chakra shifts towards letting through excess energy (and not always the good kind), you may find yourself talking too much about inconsequential matters. Unfortunately, all that talking won't allow you to listen to other people's truths either, and you'll interrupt them even when they start to reveal themselves. Even though it doesn't align with your moral compass, you may be inclined to look for gossip and pass it on, along with some negative criticism.

Knowing that this type of behavior could never make you happy wears you down, leading to many health issues. Here is a quick rundown of physical and mental symptoms you may experience with an inactive or overactive throat chakra.

Physical Symptoms of a Blocked Throat Chakra

- Throat soreness and infections
- Dental issues
- Dizziness and fatigue
- Neck and shoulder pain
- Thyroid problems
- Headaches
- Anemia
- Mouth ulcers
- Asthma

Mental Symptoms of a Blocked Throat Chakra

- Feeling of anxiety
- Inability to communicate emotions
- Difficulty expressing your thoughts
- Low self-esteem
- Depression

What the Opening of the Throat Chakra Feels Like

Since it takes time for the air to clear your throat chakra, the opening signs of this energetic center usually appear only gradually.

Each person has different symptoms when rebalancing your chakras, and your experience may reflect the causes of the blockage and the approach you take for healing. As the energy starts to flow more freely through your throat chakra, you may notice the following:

- **Throat Starts to Clear Up:** If you previously had a chronic sore throat or issues with your vocal cords, you may notice them slowly starting to disappear. They may return occasionally but eventually will go away completely.

- **Infections:** Even if you haven't had mouth or gum diseases before, these may appear as your throat chakra is activated. As you continue the process, the infections will clear up.

- **Asthma Flare-Ups:** Asthma is a chronic condition whose symptoms often deteriorate before they start disappearing because the air traveling through your lungs aggravates the affected tissue. As your health improves, your body learns to combat this condition, and the flare-up will cease to appear.

- **Fluctuating Thyroid Functions:** As one of the most affected organs in a Vishuddha imbalance, your thyroid needs more time to heal, reflecting on your overall health. This gland produces several essential hormones that keep your body and mind healthy. The functions of everything these hormones control will fluctuate, from your heartbeat and muscle strength to your metabolism.

- **You Find It Easier to Communicate:** One of the most indicative signs of a healthier Vishuddha is the improved ability to communicate with those around you. Actively honing your communication skills will facilitate the clearing process even more.

- **Improved Listening Skills:** As the air cleanses your throat chakra, it makes you more aware of your environment. This allows you to truly listen and comprehend what others are telling you, no matter how subtly they go about it.

- **Speaking the Truth:** The more you listen to others, the more you'll notice them wanting to hear your opinions. It may come hard at first, but eventually, you'll learn how to speak your truth without hesitation or fear.
- **Leaving Out Empty Words:** This goes hand in hand with speaking the truth. You only say what you truly mean because it comes from within. You'll even find it more enjoyable to speak when your thoughts and speech become aligned.
- **Alignment of Your Mind and Heart:** In the beginning, you may find it challenging to balance what your logical mind dictates and what your heart wishes. By balancing the throat chakra, these two sides will start to work in tandem.
- **Finding Your Creativity:** Freedom of speech isn't the only outlet you'll discover for your thoughts and emotions. Whether it's painting, music, or any other art or craft, you'll find many creative ways to express yourself.
- **Improved Manifestation Skills:** Learning to communicate with people will also teach you how to manifest your desires clearly through setting goals and productivity.
- **The Pleasure of Being Heard:** Transparent communication has even more beneficial outcomes. When you see others listen and validate your opinions, this fills you with immeasurable satisfaction.
- **Varying Discomfort Levels:** At first, all these changes may heighten your distress, causing the flare-up of your symptoms. As Vishuddha starts clearing up, your discomfort slowly abates.
- **Raised Self-Confidence:** Feeling healthier and happier and communicating clearly and concisely can give your confidence an enormous boost. Making even the most dreaded decisions will become easier as you feel you can achieve whatever you set your mind to.

Yoga Sequences for the Vishuddha

An imbalanced throat chakra makes the passage of energy through its center almost impossible, leaving it without spiritual nourishment. The yoga poses and the accompanying mudras allow you to relax your mind and body and provide the vital energy they need. This is achieved by opening up the airways and pushing the air through your body after each inhalation. As the oxygen-packed air passes through your throat, it will cleanse everything in its path, including Vishuddha.

Balasana

Child's pose.

Balasana, or the Child's pose, is one of the most accommodating poses to start opening your throat chakra. It relaxes the entire body, so you don't put too much pressure on your throat and neck at once. Here is how to do it:

1. Sit on your knees on a yoga mat. Place your palms on the floor on either side of your legs.
2. Inhale and raise your hands up until they reach ear level, then start lowering them down by extending them in front of you
3. Keeping your spine straight, lower yourself until your forehead and palms touch the ground.

4. Turn your head to one side and then to the other one and feel how your neck muscles start expanding.
5. Maintain the pose for 30 seconds or until you are comfortable with it and can still breathe normally. The longer you hold it, the more beneficial it will be for your throat chakra.

Bhujangasana

Cobra pose.

Kennguru, CC BY 3.0 <https://creativecommons.org/licenses/by/3.0>, via Wikimedia Commons: https://commons.wikimedia.org/wiki/File:Bhujangasana_Yoga-Asana_Nina-Mel.jpg

Bhujangasana, or the Cobra pose, is a great transition from the previous one. It's designed to stretch the spine and connect the pathways leading up to your throat. Here is how to perform this pose:

1. Take a deep breath, lay down on your stomach, then release the air from your lungs using your diaphragm.
2. Place your hand beside either side of your head with your palm facing the ground.
3. Inhale deeply once again, and start elevating your head from the ground.
4. By activating your core and taking pressure off your wrist, lift your chest as well.
5. Keep the pose for 5 to 10 breaths before returning to your initial facedown position with a deep exhalation.

Matsyasana

Fish pose.

Also known as the Fish pose, Matsyasana works similarly to the previous one. The only difference is that this pose puts more strain on the throat chakra due to the reverse neck position, awakening the connection with the upper and lower chakras. Here are the steps for this pose:

1. Start by lying flat on your back with your arms by your side, and take a deep breath.
2. After releasing the air from your lungs, move your hands higher to level your forearms with your ribcage.
3. With another inhale and putting your body weight onto your arms, lift your upper body from the ground.
4. Move your head back until you feel your throat muscles stretching.
5. Maintain the position for at least 5 breaths or for as long as possible.

Salamba Sarvangasana

Supported shoulder stand.

Salamba Sarvangasana, or supported shoulder stand, is another great exercise to awaken your throat chakra. Through the following steps, it will activate all your muscles and nerve connection in your neck, throat, and spine:

1. Lie down on your back with your arms by your side, palms facing upwards.
2. Take a deep breath. As you release it, lift your hips and legs as quickly and as high as possible.
3. Put your arms on the underside of your hips to support your weight.
4. Hold the position for 5 to 10 breaths and slowly release when finished.

Halasana

Plow pose.

Also referred to as the Plow pose, this exercise is one of the advanced techniques that may take some time to master. When you do, your entire spine becomes stronger, facilitating the travel of vital energy through your body. Here is how to form this pose:

1. Lie on your back and bring your knees towards your chest.
2. Next, straighten your knees and lift your legs towards the sky.
3. Put your arm on your lower back for initial support as you lower your legs over your head.
4. Keep your legs straight, your feet flexed, and try to reach the floor with your toes.
5. When you feel your balance has shifted back to your legs, place your hands on the ground.
6. Hold the position for 5 breaths and release with a long and steady exhale.

Ustrasana

Camel pose.

Ustrasana, or Camel pose, is another technique that promotes deep concentration and a fully relaxed body. Here are the steps for this final pose:

1. Kneel on a mat with your thighs perpendicular to the floor.
2. Move your knees hip-width apart and rotate your thighs inwardly.
3. Narrow your hips but without pressing your glutes, then press the top of your feet into the mat.
4. Place your hands on the center of your lower back to support your weight.
5. Take a deep breath and move your shoulder blades closer together.
6. Exhale and lean back as much as your back allows without straining it or releasing the tendon from your shoulders and hips.
7. With your left hand, try reaching your left heel. Bending your neck will help you with this motion and bring you to the focal point of the exercise.
8. Repeat the stretching on the other side.

Seeing as the throat chakra influences the neck, throat, and mouth areas, it stands to reason that the poses in this sequence focus on these specific regions. As you can see, most of them are geared towards strengthening this area of your body, with or without involving other organs or organ systems. Some of the poses complement each other, and you can even alternate them for better results. For example, the frequent alternation of the Cobra pose and the Fish pose is recommended for beginners wanting to train their bodies to work more intensely on the throat chakra. Both of these poses should be maintained for only a short time to not weaken your body. Besides, taking it slow and alternating them will allow you to get used to them more quickly.

Some poses should be held for 30 seconds or more, which is not always feasible for newbies with low fitness levels or those suffering from chronic, debilitating conditions. If you can't maintain a pose for as long as instructed, feel free to do it as long as your body allows it. Repeat the short sessions several times. The more times you do it, the more your endurance levels will build up, allowing you to hold the pose longer with each try. As you won't put additional stress on your body, the results will appear much sooner.

After learning about the blockage of the throat chakra, you become more aware of its tell-tale signs. As these vary and fluctuate even during the recovery process, you may find it challenging to witness any improvements. Don't be discouraged if you aren't able to perceive any positive changes at first. They may need more time to show up, or you may need to pay more close attention to them. It may also be a good idea to switch up your throat chakra clearing routine to see if there is one that works better for you. Apart from the yoga and breathing techniques, you can also try mindfulness techniques, communication exercises, or even walks in clear air to clear up Vishuddha. While this may sound like an exhausting and complex process, it doesn't necessarily have to be. It's only a matter of finding what works for you. Invariably, learning how to communicate will grant you a happier and healthier lifestyle, making all your efforts worth it.

Chapter 8: Open Your Third Eye Chakra

Also known as Ajna chakra, the third eye chakra is one of the most fundamental chakras and is associated with clairvoyance or sixth sense. The Sanskrit words roughly translate to perception and command. The third eye chakra is also referred to as the seat of intuition. Located in the very center of the forehead, right between the eyebrows, it rules over a person's wisdom and conscience.

This energy center is the highest chakra of the human body and gives us the ability to self-reflect and think with a higher level of consciousness. According to tantric philosophy, the three chakras located at the top of the human body are considered the head of the chakra sensations. In contrast, the lower chakras are considered the body. Associated with the color indigo, the third eye chakra has feminine energy and is majorly associated with light and illumination. Its symbol is a lotus flower in an upside-down triangle.

Anatomically speaking, the position of the third eye chakra is right near the pineal gland, located at the center of the brain. This gland is responsible for regulating female hormones and melatonin, which regulates sleep cycles. While no significant research proves both are connected, the third eye chakra is most significant when in a dream state, and the pineal gland connects it to that.

There can be many signs your third eye chakra is blocked, resulting in various physical, emotional, and spiritual problems.

This chapter will explain how the third eye chakra works and how you can open your third eye to manifest its full energy.

A Blocked Third Eye Chakra

A blocked chakra can cause extreme imbalance among the seven chakras and precipitate various symptoms. Physical symptoms can manifest as headaches, blurred vision, tension near the brow area, dizziness, eye strain, hearing problems, and sinus issues. In parallel, mental problems like insomnia, confusion, trouble concentrating, nightmares, and mental fog can be observed when the third eye chakra is blocked. You might be doubting yourself more than usual or overthinking excessively when this chakra is imbalanced. Spiritually, you might feel lost or misguided. Other symptoms can include:

- Feelings of purposelessness and worthlessness
- Rejection of anything beyond usual
- Inability to create a long-term plan or roadmap
- Narrow mindedness
- Lack of clarity

What Can the Third Eye Chakra Do?

Buddhists view the third eye chakra as the eye of consciousness due to the level of awareness it can lead to. The third eye chakra can be mastered for several supernatural feats, chief of which include:

- Clairvoyance
- Psychic abilities
- Manifestation
- Astral projection
- Visualization

Benefits of a Balanced Third Eye Chakra

While a blocked chakra can induce negative symptoms and side effects, many benefits come with it when balanced or opened. Whether the chakra is misaligned, aligned, or underactive, its effects can vary. When its blockages are cleared, the energy is allowed to flow smoothly through all your chakras, and as a result, you find yourself more active and present at the moment. Other benefits include:

- Mental clarity
- Improved focus
- Insight
- Decisiveness
- Enhanced intuition

How to Open Your Third Eye Chakra

While many traditions emphasize the need to work on other chakras before opening your third eye chakra, there's no hard and fast rule to this. However, it is best to balance all the other chakras before first activating the third eye chakra, as it can be somewhat destabilizing. Clearing the other chakras will help you get the grounding and capacity needed to handle the awareness that comes with the higher consciousness of the third eye. Once you feel you're ready to gain higher consciousness, try the following techniques to balance and activate your third eye chakra for enhanced insight.

1. **Use Diet Supplements**

Your diet can play a significant role in blocking or activating your chakras. Certain diet supplements promote balancing your third eye chakra more than others. Food items that can help detoxify the third eye include:

- Lemon
- Garlic
- Watermelon
- Coconut oil
- Raw cacao
- Honey
- Star anise
- Hemp seeds
- Ginseng
- Cilantro

Vitamin D3

These food items can serve to detoxify the pineal gland, which helps clear the third eye chakra from any blockages.

2. Try Essential Oils

Essential oils have been used for healing purposes for centuries and have proven effective in managing various health and spiritual problems. Many people suggest using essential oils to open up the pineal gland and the third eye chakra. The recommended essential oils for opening up the third eye chakra can include:

Lemon

Jasmine

Sandalwood

You can also create an essential oil blend using one or more of these essential oils in combination with a carrier oil. It's important to use carrier oils (olive, jojoba, coconut, sweet almond) rather than applying the essential oils directly onto your skin, as they can cause skin reactions.

To make the blend, add one teaspoon of the carrier oil with 6 drops of essential oil of your choice. Apply this mixture directly between your eyebrows, where your third eye chakra is located.

3. Incorporate Healing Crystals in Your Life

Crystals have healing powers beyond our understanding. They generate energy on a hidden frequency and significantly affect our energies. Healing crystals have been used to balance chakras for centuries. However, it's important to know which crystals can specifically help activate, balance, align and nurture the third eye chakra. Experts suggest gemstones and crystals in the violet, indigo, and purple color palette will be more effective for activating the third eye chakra. These can include:

Rhodonite

Purple Sapphire

Sodalite

Purple Fluorite

Lapis Lazuli

Clear Quartz

Citrine

Moonstone

Kyanite

Amethyst

Violet Tourmaline

To cleanse your third eye chakra using these crystals, try these tips:

During meditation, place a healing crystal on your third eye.

Wear these crystals as jewelry, especially close to the third eye chakra.

Practice positive affirmations while holding healing crystals in your fist.

Place a crystal underneath your pillow before sleeping to help awaken visions.

4. Try Sungazing

Sungazing is a unique spiritual meditation technique that involves gazing lightly at the sun when it rises and right before it sets. This technique is said to help activate the third eye chakra and increase clarity and spiritual connection. The sun is a great source of healing energy that can help cleanse your pineal gland to activate the third eye chakra. However, make sure you take proper safety precautions to avoid damaging your eyes. Wear protective gear like UV-blocking sunglasses or a face shield before looking directly at the sun, and avoid doing so for more than a few seconds at a time.

5. Meditation And Yoga

Yoga and meditation are by far the most effective ways to activate a chakra, and the third eye chakra is no exception. The pineal gland can be activated by vibrations produced during meditative rituals. In parallel, yoga can help visualize the spiritual detoxification of the third eye chakra. Specifically, holistic yoga practices can be quite cleansing for your third eye chakra. They include both asana and pranayama techniques to help guide your energy through the third eye.

Yoga Sequence

Yoga sequences designed to open the third eye chakra usually involve working on the brow area near the pineal gland. By releasing the tightness and blockages present in your body, you can physically cleanse your chakras. Here are some yoga sequences you can perform to activate your third eye chakra:

Halasana - Plough Pose

Plough pose.

This pose can help stretch the shoulders, spine, and back of the legs. It stimulates the abdominal organs, but it also helps balance the thyroid and pineal gland. Follow these steps to practice the Halasana pose:

1. Lie straight on a yoga mat with your legs outstretched and your arms near your body. Slowly exhale and push your lower back into the floor; inhale and lift your legs upward.
2. Bring your legs over your head and use this momentum to lift up your lower back off the floor. The weight should now be on your upper back and shoulders.
3. Stretch your legs as high as possible and bring your elbows close to your head. Place your palms on your lower back to keep it upright.

4. Now, move your legs over your head and towards the floor. Your heels should be touching the floor. Lift up your chin and keep your hands on your lower back to support your position.
5. Keep your spine straight and breathe deeply. Take 5 to 10 breaths in this position, then release your hands and slowly bring your legs back down.

Adho Mukha Svanasana - Downward-Facing Dog

Downward facing dog.

Besides encouraging proper blood flow, this pose can help strengthen the whole body. It is also popular for calming the mind and body. Follow these steps to practice the Adho Mukha Svanasana pose:

1. Get into an all-fours position. Make sure your hips are above your knees, and your shoulders stay above your wrists.

2. Move your hands slightly ahead of your shoulders and spread your fingers forward. Press the other edge of your palm and fingers on the floor, creating a suction cup in the middle of your hands.
3. Roll your upper arms away from your shoulders and bring your forearms inwards. This will create a spiraling action in your arms.
4. Now, exhale slowly and bring the navel back to the spine to bring yourself into an upside-down V-pose.
5. Your knees will be bent at first, so stretch them completely until you're at your maximum height while bending downwards.
6. Spread your collarbones while keeping your neck relaxed. Now, gently bend and straighten your legs. Do this for 5 to 10 breaths, and slowly release the pose.

Balasana - Child Pose

Child's pose.

As one of the easiest yoga poses, the Balasana pose can effectively help you stretch your lower body. It relieves fatigue and acts as a calming pose for the body and mind. Follow these simple steps to practice the child pose:

1. Sit on the yoga mat with your heels facing the floor, and slowly bring your face towards the ground.
2. You can either keep your hands stretched out to the front or underneath your forehead to shield your face.

3. You'll notice your third eye chakra touching the ground. Relax into this pose and breathe in and out.
4. Stay like this for several minutes to rest your mind completely and cleanse your third eye chakra.

Padmasana - Lotus Pose

Lotus pose.

The Lotus pose is a special pranayama and asana technique that strengthens your muscles while detoxifying your chakras. Follow these steps to practice the Padmasana pose:

1. Get into a cross-legged position and gently straighten your spine while you inhale.
2. Slowly exhale and move your right leg as far out as possible. Bring the thigh and calf together to close the knee.
3. Now, bring the outer side of the right foot to the inner left groin as you inhale.
4. Move your left leg over the right, and bring it in the same position as the right leg to rest in your inner right groin.
5. Bring your knees as close together as possible.
6. Place your hands on your knees with the palms facing upwards. Curl your thumbs and index fingers to touch

each other.

7. Stretch your spine until it is completely straightened. Take 10 deep breaths while reciting affirmations to cleanse your third eye chakra and bring clarity to your mind.

Viparita Karani - Legs Up the Wall Pose

Legs Up The Wall

Viparita Karani.

This yoga pose is a popular choice for those seeking to relax their mind and body. It is a restorative pose in nature and is easily modifiable. Follow these steps to practice the Viparita Karani pose:

1. Sit with the wall to your right, your knees bent and feet drawn inwards.
2. Lie flat on the ground, swing your legs towards the wall, and let them rest there.
3. Now, place your hips against the wall to balance your body. Get your arms in a comfortable position near your body.
4. Maintain this position for 10 to 20 minutes.

5. To exit this pose, slowly move away from the wall, draw your knees close to your chest, and roll to the side. This will reinvigorate your body and soothe your spirit.

Baddha Virabhadrasana - Humble Warrior Pose

Humble warrior pose.

This pose promotes clarity of mind and circulation for a healthier body. Follow these steps to practice the Humble Warrior pose:

1. Stand with your feet together and your arms alongside your body. Your feet should be a hip distance apart.
2. Exhale slowly, move your left leg to the back, and bend this leg at a 45-degree angle.
3. Bring the right foot to the front and bend it at a 90-degree angle to kneel on one leg.
4. Make sure you distribute your weight evenly on your feet. Now, stretch out the back leg as much as you can.
5. Slowly inhale and bring your arms over your head. Stretch your collar bones apart and lengthen the tailbone.
6. Now, circle the arms behind your back and interlace your fingers. Exhale slowly and bring your hands towards the sky.
7. Keep your head bent towards the ground and stay in this position for 5 to 8 breaths.

Prasarita Padottanasana - Wide-Legged Forward Pose

Wide-legged forward pose.

This calming yoga pose can help relieve stress, headaches, and backaches. It is especially popular for opening up a blocked third eye chakra. Follow these steps to practice the Prasarita Padottanasana pose:

1. Start by facing the length of your yoga mat in the Mountain pose. Keep your feet wide apart and place your hands on your hips.
2. Keep your spine straight while you bend slowly over your legs. Don't let your back bend even slightly while you do this.
3. Now, place your hands flat on the floor to the front, and stretch your torso forward.
4. Gently bend forward until your head touches the floor while still keeping your spine straight. Your legs should be firmly planted on the ground.
5. Take a few deep breaths and straighten your arms. Slowly inhale and lift your body back upwards to exit the pose.

Ardha Pincha Mayurasana - Dolphin Pose

Dolphin pose.

The Dolphin pose is a super popular yoga pose to open up the body's various chakras. It helps you gain confidence and insight you normally wouldn't have. Here's how you can practice the Dolphin pose:

1. Get on all fours on a comfortable yoga mat, with your arms under your shoulders and knees beneath your hips.
2. Place your elbows on the ground slightly apart, and interlace your fingers together.
3. Press down onto your forearms to move your shoulders away from your face.
4. Exhale slowly and move your hips upwards to allow your head to hang freely.

5. Slowly move your shoulder blades into your chest to improve circulation.
6. Lengthen your spine and keep your knees straight. Stay in this position for 5 to 10 breaths.
7. Bring your knees to the floor and release your hands to exit this position.

Ustrasana - Camel Pose

Lastly, while the Camel pose is known for opening the heart chakra, it can also serve to unblock the third eye chakra. Here's how you can practice the Camel pose:

1. Get into a kneeling position with your body upright and your hips placed above your knees.
2. Expand your chest towards the ceiling to open up the chakra paths.
3. Use your hands to grab your heels and tuck your toes under your heels.
4. Bring your hips forward and position them over the knees.
5. Lift up your head towards the ceiling. This will also open up your throat chakra.
6. Stay in this position for 5 to 10 breaths, then release by bringing your face back down. Gently bring your body back to the initial upright kneeling position.

The third eye chakra is one of the most important upper body chakras, and its blockages can severely affect your overall well-being. Not only can an obstructed third eye chakra hinder your intellectual capabilities, but it can induce certain physical side effects. For that reason, it is essential to cleanse, align, and open up the third eye chakra for a balanced chakra system. As we've seen, you can do this through various techniques, including supplementing your diet, sungazing, using healing crystals, or meditating and practicing holistic yoga techniques. The included yoga sequence has been shown to help clear third eye chakra blockages and heal your mind and body. Now that you know how to restore balance to this vital energy center, we're ready to move on to awakening the crown chakra.

Chapter 9: Awaken the Crown Chakra

Sahasrara is the Sanskrit name for the crown chakra, and it means "thousand-petalled." As the last of the seven chakras, it is associated with spirituality, enlightenment, connection, and consciousness. It is the center of our wisdom, given its location right above the crown of the head. The chakra's location links it to the brain and nervous system, making it responsible for our intelligence. Sahasrara is also closely connected to the first root chakra since both serve as "bookends" for the chakras. The chakra system begins with one and ends with the other.

The energy of this chakra radiates on top of the head, resembling a crown. It is often considered the bridge to the cosmos and plays a vital role in human spirituality. In fact, Sahasrara stands out from all the other chakras as the most spiritual and one that can help you connect with the divine and your higher self. Through the crown chakra and reaching a higher state of consciousness, you can experience spiritual growth.

Your truest potential lies in the crown chakra, as it plays a central role in how you communicate with the universe to lead a healthy spiritual life. It is sometimes regarded as an umbilical cord connecting us to the divine. It allows us to experience unity with a higher power and the universe around us. The universe is an expansion of the same energy we are made of. One can experience true bliss as the consciousness moves up to the top of their head. That is the moment you realize you are truly one with the universe. You are no longer conflicted about your place in the universe since you are now at one. This unity makes you lose interest in the materialistic world, as you connect with something bigger than yourself. As a result, you experience wisdom, clarity, and enlightenment.

Made of masculine energy, Sahasrara is represented by the color purple. This chakra's symbol is a lotus with a thousand petals symbolizing the divine, and its mantra is "I know." The most dominant feeling when this chakra is awakened is gratitude. Unlike the other chakras, the crown chakra doesn't have an element. This is what makes it quite unique. It is considered pure spirit and energy that transcends the physical world, and therefore it can't be associated with an element.

The crown chakra is also the meeting point of the seven chakras, where the energies meet when they travel up the spine. You shouldn't attempt to open Sahasrara before you awaken all the other chakras first. Having a fully open crown chakra feels like no other, one that only very few can experience.

Our planet has its own crown chakra, located in Mount Kailash in Tibet and considered one of its most sacred mountains. In fact, the Tibetans prohibit anyone from climbing it and consider the mere thought offensive to the divine. This mountain is usually referred to as "the roof of the world," which is only befitting for the Earth's crown chakra.

The Function of the Crown Chakra

The crown chakra connects you with the divine to make you experience feelings of enlightenment, self-realization, devotion, and wisdom. Establishing a connection with a divine source can grant you abundant healing energy that you can dip into whenever your spirit is struggling. When the Sahasrara is awakened, you can connect to your higher self through its energy.

The crown chakra also governs certain vital areas in your life, such as spirituality, fulfillment, consciousness, and your life's purpose. It increases your awareness and opens your eyes to the fact that life is more than just fulfilling our earthly needs. It helps you see yourself beyond your physical body and look into your soul to experience your own divinity.

In short, the crown chakra helps you answer the age-old question: Who are you? Why are you here? Once you answer these mysteries for yourself, you begin to live a life of purpose and unleash your truest potential.

What Causes a Blocked Sahasrara

The crown chakra can get blocked for several reasons. When its energy is stagnant, it will disrupt your body's balance and manifest itself through various emotional, physical, and mental symptoms. Emotional distress is one of the main causes of a blocked crown chakra. If you experience a loss or an accident that impacts your emotional wellness, this may throw Sahasrara out of balance. Negative emotions we experience every day like worry, stress, fear, and internal conflict, but also the illness can disrupt the crown chakra's flow of energy.

An Imbalanced Crown Chakra

The crown chakra detaches you from the materialistic world and brings you closer to the universe. Your crown chakra's energy is likely stuck when you feel you are only concerned with materialistic pursuits and unwilling to change your attitude or mindset. You'll also feel disconnected from your surroundings and dissociated from your body. Your outlook towards life will also change as pessimism and uncontrollable negative thoughts begin to plague your existence.

Since it connects you to the divine, an imbalanced crown chakra can make you doubt the idea of a higher power. Some people can be slightly skeptical, whereas others will experience extreme skepticism and reject the idea of a supreme god entirely. They usually feel alone and abandoned since they don't connect with the universe or the spiritual realm. They wonder how there could be a higher power when injustice and evil are so prevalent in this world, leading to feelings of anger and resentfulness in the end.

These sentiments will then expand until these individuals start to develop a selfish attitude and grow detached from humanity altogether. They don't feel any connection to the people in their lives, treating them as a means to an end. Everyone else must be controlled, managed, tolerated, and defended against if necessary. Down the line, this can result in isolation, boredom, and profound disillusion.

The more a person gives in to the materialistic world and relinquishes the spiritual realm, the more they develop negative traits like greed and damaging behavior. They become overly attached to their material possessions and value themselves by what they own, wear, where they hang out, and with who. Their lives revolve around what grants them status, like the latest luxury car or marrying a successful partner. They believe they are nothing without these things and are convinced their happiness depends on them. To them, only money buys happiness, blatantly unaware that true happiness lies within.

Under these conditions, awakening the crown chakra can be very challenging. After all, how can someone who is so detached from the spiritual world believe that a blocked chakra is the root of their affliction? In fact, their skepticism can reach an alarming level of condescension, sarcasm, and narrow-mindedness towards anything related to spirituality.

They tend to dismiss anything they can't sense with their five senses. At the root, their spirit may be suffering, but they are unaware of it because the concept of a spiritual world is so foreign to them. What their spirit is feeling will resurface as mental or physical symptoms.

Owing to their disbelief, they will be reluctant to engage in spiritual activities like meditation or yoga. On some occasions, their relationships may suffer, especially if they have friends or family members who are spiritual. So, their inability to project themselves or empathize with different beliefs may cause discord in their relationships.

Do you feel like drama always follows you wherever you go? You may think it isn't your fault. However, in some cases, people with blocked chakras usually have constant drama in their lives. This can result from their stubbornness or patronizing attitude regarding things they don't particularly understand or believe in.

Being disconnected from the universe, they may be unable to look beyond the world they have created for themselves. They are unaware of the universe's size and don't know the first thing about the spiritual world. For this reason, they have a narrow, rigid perspective of the world.

Physical Symptoms of a Blocked Crown Chakra

Certain physical symptoms manifest when your crown chakra is blocked, chief of which include:

- Headaches and migraines
- Pituitary gland issues
- Imbalance
- Altered physical function
- Poor coordination
- Hair loss
- Amnesia
- Chronic fatigue

Mental Symptoms of a Blocked Crown Chakra

You may also experience one or more of these mental symptoms:

- Lack of focus
- Disconnection from the world
- Lack of empathy
- Destructive behavior
- Depression and anxiety
- Confusion and distraction
- Controlling behavior
- Mental fog
- Narcissism
- Altered cognitive function
- Greed

- Superiority
- Feeling abandoned
- Cynicism

What a Balanced Crown Chakra Feels Like

As your crown chakra opens, you'll experience new and positive feelings. A blocked chakra throws the mind into chaos, so feelings of calmness and peace wash over you when it awakens. Feelings of anxiety, anger, or frustration no longer consume you because you aren't focused on the past or concerned with the future. You simply live in the present moment. You begin to develop a deeper connection with the universe and all its beings, and your awareness of the spiritual world grows with each passing day. The materialistic world no longer holds much importance to you as you begin to strive for better, more significant ideals. Instead of greed, you become content and understand that true happiness lies inside you, not in your possessions.

Chances are that big life changes will be in order. People who experience an awakening in their crown chakra have changed their careers, lifestyle, and beliefs. Their priorities shift as they are no longer concerned with materialism. They begin to experience spiritual growth and enlightenment and acquire self-knowledge and precious wisdom as they turn their focus to the spiritual world and the divine.

The knowledge and wisdom they gain will help them develop a better understanding of the physical world to better overcome daily obstacles. They will develop a positive attitude towards life because they know they aren't afraid to handle whatever life throws at them.

Opening the crown chakra will pave the way to finding and connecting with a higher power. You won't feel bitter when something doesn't go as planned because you know everything happens for a reason. You'll become more giving and loving towards the people in your life. As your crown chakra opens up, so will your mind. You'll be able to see things from a different perspective and understand that others can have radically different opinions and beliefs from your own. You become more understanding and accepting of differences.

You see the work of divine power in everything and everyone around you, which will grant you a positive outlook on life. When your crown chakra is fully open, you'll be in a state of bliss, joy, and serene peace.

Yoga Sequence for the Crown Chakra

Opening your root chakra is possible, and one of the most effective ways to unblock Sahasrara is, you might have guessed, yoga. Follow these steps to guarantee the best results, and remember to focus on your breathing.

Headstand – Shirshasana

Headstand.

This is the ideal yoga posture for awakening the crown chakra. It also improves your balance, provides clarity, increases your strength, and boosts your energy. We recommend you remain in this pose for at least five breaths.

1. First, measure the ideal distance by sitting on your knees and holding your elbows.
2. Next, move your arms to the ground, right under your shoulders.
3. Without moving your elbows, bring your hands closer together and interlock your fingers (your arms should be forming a triangle shape). Make sure your elbows don't spread outwards.

4. Place your head on the ground and ensure the back of the head is in your hands.
5. Curl your toes, keep your knees straight, and your hips pointing upwards.
6. Moving towards your shoulders, bring your right knee to your chest and your left knee towards the chest while keeping your spine straight.
7. Raise your legs while you inhale.
8. Keep your feet in front of you while straightening your legs upward.
9. Keep your focus on a fixed point at eye level.
10. Breathe gently and remain as relaxed as possible.
11. Remain in this posture for as long as you can.

Rabbit Pose - Sasangasana

Rabbit pose.

This pose will help you connect with the crown chakra, allowing you to relax your sounders, head, and spine in the process.

1. Kneel and bow forward to bring the crown of your head towards the ground.
2. Hold your knees from behind with your hands and wrists.
3. Gently touch the ground with your head.
4. Take a few deep breaths and relax.
5. Lower your hips towards your heels, let go of your heels and return to a seated position to exit the pose.

Corpse Pose - Savasana

The corpse pose is considered one of the simplest and most effective yoga exercises. It can help you let go of judgments, desires, and expectations. To connect with your crown chakra, it helps to practice visualization. Picture a white light entering your body from the crown of your head, flowing down through your spine as you inhale. As you breathe out, visualize the white light moving up your spine back to the crown of your head.

1. Lie down on your back.
2. Spread your arms and legs on the floor (with your arms approximately 45 degrees from your body).
3. Close your eyes. Breathe in and out slowly and deeply through your nose.
4. Relax into the ground and feel your body become heavy and soft.
5. As you relax, feel how your body moves with every inhale.
6. Feel every part of your body, starting with your toes all the way up to the crown of your head, and scan for tightness or tension. Rock your body from side to side to release any tension.
7. Let go of any control, whether in your body, mind, or breath. Allow yourself to enter a state of deep relaxation.
8. Remain in this position for 5 to 10 minutes.
9. Take slow and deep breaths, wiggle your toes and fingers, reach your arms over your head, and stretch to exit this position. Breathe out, bring your knees towards your chest,

and roll over into a fetus position. Remain as such until you feel ready, breathe in slowly, and return to a seated position.

Lotus Pose - Padmasana

Lotus pose.

Bryan Helfrich, Alias52, CC BY-SA 3.0 <https://creativecommons.org/licenses/by-sa/3.0>, via Wikimedia Commons: https://commons.wikimedia.org/wiki/File:Lotus_position.svg

This is a very simple yoga pose, ideal for awakening the root chakra. While practicing, only focus on your root chakra.

1. Sit on the floor with your legs extended (Dandasana position).
2. Bend your right knee out to your side and cradle your foot and knee in your hands. Then, rotate your left leg from the hip area, and bring your foot to the crease of your left hip.
3. Bend your left knee and rotate the thigh outward from the hip.
4. Slowly lift your shin and bring your left foot over the right one to tuck into the crease of your right hip.
5. Rest the tops of both feet against your upper thighs, then release your knees towards the floor.

6. Sit up straight, preferably on a folded blanket, to prevent spine rounding.
7. Inhale and exhale slowly and deeply.
8. Remain in this position for as long as you can.

Crocodile Pose – Makarasana

Crocodile pose.

This last exercise will help you relax your whole body. You can also try visualization while practicing. Throughout the session, focus intently on the connection between your body and the universe.

1. Lie down on your stomach.
2. Bend your right leg back to form a 45-degree angle with your calf and thigh.
3. Keep your left leg straight.
4. Relax your left cheek on the mat and gaze to your right.
5. Create a pillow by placing your hands under your left cheek.
6. Take slow and deep breaths.
7. Remain in this position for 10 minutes and repeat with the other leg.

Awakening the crown chakra can transform your life in powerful ways, but this is the last chakra you should work on the opening. To achieve that and connect with your higher self, some of the yoga poses mentioned in this chapter are easy and ideal for beginners. Step into the spiritual world to be one with the universe and the divine by practicing this yoga sequence, and experience the pleasures of setting your Sahasrara free.

Chapter 10: Daily Yoga Routine for All Chakras

Widely considered a popular type of complementary therapy, yoga can help balance the chakras. This is because it works on aligning your body and keeping you attuned with all your physical sensations. Besides incorporating yoga into your regular practice, there are other things you can do to support the health of the chakras and encourage a smooth, balanced energetic flow throughout. Using healing stones and reciting affirmations are some examples.

In this closing chapter, you'll learn how to choose the right crystal to support the function of each chakra. Also included is a 7-day daily routine chart detailing daily yoga sequences. Each day is dedicated to healing one of the chakras and comes with an affirmation that you can recite throughout your daily practice.

Choosing the Right Healing Stone

Each chakra corresponds to a certain set of healing stones. Since each crystal has its own unique energy, it is necessary to understand what you plan to do with it, what the healing stone can do, and which chakra you wish to balance. Otherwise, you won't be able to achieve the desired results. That said, some chakras have healing stones in common. As a reminder and starting point, it helps to know the colors associated with each chakra:

The root chakra: Red

The sacral chakra: Orange

The solar plexus chakra: Yellow

The heart chakra: Green

The throat chakra: Blue

The third eye chakra: Indigo

The crown chakra: Violet/Purple

Here are some healing stones you can use for each chakra. Notice how the colors of most healing stones match the colors of their chakras:

Root Chakra

- Garnet

Garnets are potent healing crystals that carry high vibrations. Using them will help you instill your trust in others, yourself, and your instincts. They can also help refine your survival instinct and encourage you to make challenging decisions.

- Bloodstone

Bloodstones are known for their immense healing powers. They work great for resolving problems associated with the root chakra, such as financial literacy and monetary anxiety. This stone is also used to promote better self-confidence and self-esteem.

- Red Aventurine

Red Aventurine is associated with manifestation, prosperity, success, and luck. Using this stone can help you head toward the life you desire. It can help you turn your wishes into reality and maintain a healthy relationship with money.

Other useful stones to heal your root chakra include black tourmaline, red tiger's eye, black jasper, hematite, and black onyx.

Sacral Chakra

- Carnelian

Carnelian can help stimulate your creative and passionate energies. It is the ideal stone for a boost of enthusiasm. Carnelian is known to help us achieve a more joyful state of mind. Associated with feminine energy, it also assists with the menstrual cycle.

- **Citrine**

Citrine is associated with financial abundance and prosperity. It can also bolster one's confidence and creative powers.

- **Moonstone**

Moonstone serves to ameliorate a person's sense of creativity and intuition. It is also believed to aid with menstrual cramps. This stone is incredibly powerful because it shares the same vibrational energy with the moon. It can help attract positive experiences into your life.

Jasper, tiger's eye, smoky quartz, and coral are some other healing crystals that can help balance the sacral chakra.

Solar Plexus Chakra

- **Citrine**

Citrines are associated with confidence, balance, and luck. They can help you feel empowered and cleanse your energy. This is the perfect stone when it comes to replenishing your life with positive energies and promoting joy and happiness. This stone is believed to bring the most auspicious energy.

- **Amber**

Ambers are renowned for their cleansing and balancing properties, and they can help you gain better mental clarity and become more self-confident. These healing crystals are great for healing mental, emotional, and physical health imbalances.

- **Calcite**

Calcite, metaphorically speaking, can turn ashes into gold. This stone can turn even the smallest pinch of power and positivity into an abundance of charm, vitality, and confidence. It is ideal for those who wish to come out of their shell or break patterns of behavior that no longer serve them.

Other gemstones associated with the solar plexus chakra include ametrine, yellow jasper, rutilated quartz, and yellow quartz.

Heart Chakra

- **Rose Quartz**

Rose Quartz will serve to overcome emotional challenges and traumas. Its energy is incredibly soothing, meaning it can help you endure tough periods in your life. This healing stone carries tender, pure, compassionate, nourishing, and peaceful energies that can help you deal with grief, break-ups, or other major life changes.

- **Rhodochrosite**

Rhodochrosite is great for emotional healing and boosting one's self-esteem. It also promotes self-love and can help you gain greater control over your feelings and emotions. You can use it to achieve forgiveness and compassion.

- **Aventurine**

Aventurine is the perfect stone for those who tend to listen to their minds more than they listen to their hearts. It can help you live your best life and peacefully let go of relationships that no longer serve you.

Healing crystals like emerald, aquamarine, amazonite, green quartz, and jade are also helpful for the heart chakra.

Throat Chakra

- **Lapis Lazuli**

If you struggle with public speaking, then Lapis Lazuli is your stone. This dazzling blue-shaded healing crystal can help you communicate openly and clearly. It can also allow you to cultivate and maintain strong social networks and bring your ideas to life. Use this stone whenever you need to set a remarkable first impression.

- **Blue Apatite**

Blue Apatite can help you attract joy and happiness into your mind and is also used to achieve mental clarity and better self-expression. It can rid you of pessimism and emotional burnout and boost your enthusiasm and independence.

- **Blue Kyanite**

This healing crystal can mitigate mental, spiritual, and physical blockages. It can raise your communication abilities to a higher vibrational level and promote inner peace and tranquility. Combine this stone with other throat chakra gemstones for the best results.

Blue quartz, blue tiger's eye, blue goldstone, sodalite, labradorite, and aquamarine can also support your throat chakra.

Third Eye Chakra

- **Amethyst**

Amethysts are widely associated with spiritual awakenings. They can help their wearers tap into their third eye and intuition. This healing crystal promotes better sleep, alleviates headaches, relieves frustration, and calms the mind.

- **Lapis Lazuli**

This healing crystal works wonders for the crown and third eye chakra, just as it does for the throat. It can help you unlock your inner intellect, tap into your intuitive and visionary powers, and achieve greater wisdom.

- **Labradorite**

Because it is also associated with the throat chakra, Labradorite ensures that what you say aligns with what you feel. It also guarantees that you see the bigger picture, recognize your inner power, and protect yourself as you exploit your psychic and intuitive powers.

Azurite, black obsidian, sodalite, and blue quartz can also help the third eye chakra.

Crown Chakra

- **Celestite**

This crystal heightens a person's intuition and helps them embark on their spiritual journey. It is also widely used to attract prosperity, stability, and tranquility in life.

- **Amethyst**

Amethyst can alleviate many physical symptoms, including pain, headaches, anxiety, and insomnia. It does so by relaxing the pineal and pituitary glands, the crown of the head, and even the entire nervous system.

- **Clear Quartz**

Finally, Clear Quartz can give you a general energetic boost, allowing you to release all blockages from your crown chakra. It will relieve symptoms associated with an imbalanced crown chakra, such as tension and exhaustion.

Ametrine, serpentine, and selenite are also helpful to the crown chakra.

Incorporating Healing Crystals Into Your Yoga Practice

When you're practicing yoga, simply place one or several healing crystals of your choice at the top of your mat. For instance, if you're working on healing the root chakra, you can use a Carnelian. If you're doing poses that involve lying down on your back, you can place the healing stone on its corresponding chakra. Let's say you're doing the Savasana, which ultimately opens the heart chakra. In that case, you can place a Celestite on your heart as you lie down. Don't hesitate to conduct further research on how crystals can help elevate your yoga sessions spiritually.

7-Day Chakra Yoga Routine

The chakra healing journey is a long and eye-opening one. You'll likely encounter many challenges along the way, especially when you spend months experimenting without achieving apparent results, which can be disheartening at times. Healing your chakras is a lot more than wearing healing stones and striking yoga poses. It's about acknowledging your traumas, unhealthy relationships, unhelpful habits, and taking action. Aligning your chakras is not a one-time thing. It takes plenty of effort to get there and even more hard work to maintain the results. You need to be consistent with your efforts, whether it's a yoga routine, long walks in nature, meditation, identifying and breaking negative patterns, or, hopefully, a combination of approaches. This is because when one of your chakras gives out, all the others will fall out of tune. What you do to nurture your chakras should be a part of your lifestyle. To achieve that - *which can never be stressed enough* - consistency and perseverance are essential.

We encourage you to practice one yoga sequence from the previous chapters, preferably in order, every single day for a week. Here's a 7-day chakra routine you can use to take things one step further. Feel free to repeat it as many times as needed:

Day 1: Root Chakra Healing

Affirmation: "I am grounded and deeply rooted."

Uttanasana - Standing Forward Bend
1. Start in Mountain Pose. Stand at the front of your mat and place your hands on your hips.
2. Slightly bend your knees before you fold your torso over. Make sure your hips are the ones folding over, not your lower back.
3. Rest your palms on the ground in front of or beside your feet.
4. Inhale, extending your spine and chest in the process.
5. Exhale, slowly springing both your legs nearly straight. Your kneecaps should be lifted, and your upper and inner thighs should go back.
6. Inhale once more and push your torso downward as you exhale. Don't round your back. Your neck should be lengthened as you draw your shoulders towards the direction of your hips.
7. Stay there for around 8 deep breaths.

Virabhadrasana I - Warrior I
1. From Uttanasana, move your arms forward and into a downward-facing dog. Stay there for a few seconds to stretch out before placing your right foot forward. Your toes should be aligned with your fingertips. Adjust your foot slightly to the right.

2. Your knees should be at a 90-degree angle and your thighs parallel to the floor.
3. Your left foot should turn to face the side of the mat. The left and right heels should be aligned. You can go wider if you're not stable enough. Keep your left knee straight.
4. On inhalation, reach up with both arms, raising your torso in the process. Keep your palms facing each other and your shoulders open. Rotate your biceps, bringing your palms together. Look up to your thumbs.
5. Keep your left thigh straight as you bring your tailbone towards the floor.
6. Hold for 5 to 10 breaths before shifting to a downward-facing dog and repeating on the other side.

Balasana - Child Pose

1. Bring yourself to your hands and knees, spreading your knees as wide apart as possible. Keep your feet on the floor and allow your big toes to touch.
2. Push your belly down to the ground and rest your forehead on the floor. Soften up your facial features.
3. Stretch your arms out in front of you, resting your palms on the floor.
4. Stay there for as long as you need to.

Day 2: Unblock Your Sacral Chakra

Affirmation: "I am able to freely and healthily express my emotions."

Utkatasana - Chair Pose

Chair pose.

1. Stand up straight and move your arms over your head as you inhale. Your palms should be facing inward.
2. On exhalation, bend your knees, keeping your thighs parallel to the floor. Your thigh bones should align with your heels, and your inner thighs should be kept parallel.
3. Your shoulder blades should be aligned with your back. Keep your tailbone pointed towards the floor.
4. Stay there for 8 breaths.

Utkata Konasana - Goddess Pose

1. Stand up straight with both feet wide apart. Point your toes outward and bend your knees so they're parallel to the floor.
2. Align your knees with the middle of your feet, and keep your shoulders above your hips.
3. Extend the crown of your head towards the sky as you point your tailbone downward.
4. Bring both palms together, parallel to the heart.
5. Stay in this position for 8 to 10 breaths.

Paripurna Navasana - Boat Pose

Boat pose.

1. Sit down with your knees bent and your feet rested on the mat.
2. Keep your hands behind your hips and lengthen your spine as you lift up your chest.
3. Keep your heart lifted while you lean back slightly. You can extend your arms in front of you and lift your shins up straight. Make sure to engage your core.
4. Stay there for 10 deep breaths.

Day 3: Activate Your Solar Plexus Chakra

Affirmation: "I let go of the need to be in control."

Paripurna Navasana - Boat Pose

1. Sit down and bend your knees. Plant your feet on the mat.
2. Place your hands behind your hips and lengthen your spine as you lift up your chest.
3. Keep your heart lifted and lean back gently.
4. Extend your arms in front of you and lift your shins up straight parallel to the floor.
5. Stay there for 10 deep breaths.

Surya Mudra - Fire Gesture

1. Stay seated and bring your hands to rest on your legs.
2. Bend your ring fingers in the direction of your palms, covering them with your thumbs.
3. Keep this position for 5 minutes and focus on your breathing.

Virabhadrasana I - Warrior I

1. Shift yourself into a downward-facing dog before moving your right foot forward, aligning your toes with your fingertips. Move your foot slightly to the right.
2. Your knees should be at a 90-degree angle and your thighs parallel to the floor.
3. Your left foot should turn to face the side of the mat. Align your left and right heels.
4. As you inhale, reach up with both arms, raising your torso in the process. Keep your palms facing each other and your shoulders open. Rotate your biceps, bringing your palms together. Look up to your thumbs.
5. Keep your left thigh straight as you bring your tailbone towards the floor.
6. Hold for 5 to 10 breaths before shifting to a downward-facing dog and repeating on the other side.

Day 4: Open Your Heart Chakra

Affirmation: "I am open to giving and receiving love."

Uttanasana - Standing Forward Bend

1. Stand straight at the front of your mat and place your hands on your hips.
2. Slightly bend your knees before you fold your hips, allowing your torso to hang over.
3. Rest your palms on the ground in front of or beside your feet.
4. Inhale as you extend your spine and chest.
5. Exhale, slowly springing both your legs nearly straight. Your kneecaps should be lifted, and your upper and inner thighs should spiral back.

6. Inhale again, and then push your torso downward as you exhale. Lengthen your neck as you draw your shoulders towards the direction of your hips.
7. Stay there for around 8 deep breaths.

Salamba Bhujangasana - Sphinx Pose
1. Lie down on your belly, placing your elbows beneath your shoulders.
2. Keep your shoulders relaxed, focusing on the lift in your chest as your shoulder blades roll down your back.
3. Notice how your breaths feel in your abdomen and lower back.
4. Focus your breathing on your abdomen and your lower back.
5. Stay there for as long as you need to.

Bhujangasana - Cobra Pose
1. From the Sphinx pose, rest your chest on the floor and move your hands to the sides of your ribs.
2. Extend your toes and rest your feet on the ground.
3. Move your inner thighs to face the ceiling, extending your lower back.
4. Press with your hands to lift your head and chest before rolling your shoulders down.
5. Keep your neck extended and your sternum lifted.
6. Straighten your arms so there's a slight bend in your elbows.
7. Stay for 10 breaths.

Day 5: Balance Your Throat Chakra

Affirmation: "I speak my truth freely."

Balasana - Child Pose
1. Bring yourself to your hands and knees, spreading your knees as wide apart as possible. Press your feet to the floor and allow your big toes to touch.

2. Rest your belly on the ground before gently planting your forehead on the floor. Relax your jaws, eyes, ears, and other tense muscles.
3. Stretch your arms out before you, resting your palms on the floor.
4. Stay there for as long as you need to.

Bhujangasana - Cobra Pose
1. Lie down on your belly, your chest on the floor, and your hands at the sides of your ribs.
2. Extend your toes and rest your feet on the ground.
3. Move your inner thighs to face the ceiling and extend your lower back.
4. Press gently with your hands to lift your head and chest before rolling your shoulders down.
5. Lift your sternum to extend your neck.
6. Straighten your arms so there's a slight bend in your elbows.
7. Stay for 10 breaths.

Salamba Sarvangasana - Supported Shoulder Stand
1. Lie down on your back and keep your arms at your sides. Your palms should face the ceiling.
2. Take a deep breath and lift your hips and legs in the process. Do it as quickly and as high as you can.
3. Rest your arms beneath your hips to support your weight.
4. Stay there for 5 to 10 breaths.

Day 6: Revive Your Third Eye Chakra

Affirmation: "I can clearly see my life's purpose."

Balasana - Child Pose
1. Bring yourself to your hands and knees with your knees far apart. Keep your feet on the floor and allow your big toes to touch.
2. Rest your belly on the ground before gently planting your forehead on the floor. Soften up your facial features.

3. Stretch your arms out before you and rest your palms on the floor.
4. Stay there for as long as you need to.

Adho Mukha Svanasana - Downward-Facing Dog

1. Bring yourself back to your hands and knees, spreading your palms and knees far apart. Align your shoulders and wrists.
2. Curl your toes under your feet and rest your palms right in front of your shoulders. They should be flat against the ground.
3. Raise your knees off the mat, forming a V-shape at the hips.
4. Keep your legs straight and your toes pointed forward. Try to reach for the mat with your heels.
5. Hold and focus on breathing deeply and steadily.
6. Hold for 5 to 10 breaths.

Ardha Uttanasana - Standing Half Forward Bend

Ardha Uttanasana.

1. From a downward-facing dog, walk your hands back to Uttanasana. Press your palms into the ground beside your feet and straighten your elbows with an inhale.
2. Arch your torso upward, creating as much length as you can.

3. Push your palms against the floor, lifting the top of your sternum forward and up. Allow your knees to bend slightly.
4. Look forward, allowing your back to arch a little.
5. Hold for 5 to 10 breaths before exiting into full Uttanasana.

Day 7: Crown Chakra Awakening

Affirmation: "I am united with the world around me."

Paschimottanasana - Seated Forward Bend

1. Sit down with your legs extended in front of you. Press your heels into the mat and keep your feet flexed. Soften your toes.
2. Inhale while you take your hands over your head with your palms facing each other. On exhalation, move your arms forward and down. Reach for your feet. When moving your upper body, lead with your heart, and don't bend your lower back first.
3. Keep your back and torso flexed.
4. Feel the stretch at the base of your spine. Stay there for 10 to 14 breaths.

Salamba Sarvangasana - Supported Shoulder Stand

1. Lie down on your back with your arms at your sides and your palms facing upward.
2. Take a deep breath and lift your hips and legs in the process. Do it as quickly and as high as you can.
3. Rest your arms underneath your hips to support your weight.
4. Stay there for 5 to 10 breaths.

Halasana - Plough Pose

1. Lie on your back with your knees bent over your chest.
2. Straighten your knees out, lifting your legs upward and towards the sky.
3. Place your hands on your lower back for support, and lower your legs over your head.

4. Your legs should be straight, and your feet flexed. Reach for the floor with your toes.
5. If you're balanced enough, place your hands on the ground.
6. Stay there for 5 breaths before releasing on an exhale.

Ultimately, your subtle body can regain its balance through specific yoga postures whose purpose is to maintain a sense of balance and stability in your physical being. Your chakras automatically realign in the process, causing them to strengthen. This can help you overcome various unhelpful or toxic behaviors, letting go of patterns, values, thoughts, emotions, and beliefs that no longer serve you. Eventually, your chakras will fall back into balance, and you'll experience a blissful sense of unity between mind, body, and soul.

Extra: Quiz — Which of My Chakras Need Yoga Balancing?

The following quiz can help you determine which of your chakras is out of balance:

1. **What is your least favorite color?**
    a. Red
    b. Orange
    c. Yellow
    d. Green
    e. Blue
    f. Indigo
    g. Violet
2. **How would you like someone to describe you?**
    a. I'd like people to think I'm grounded.
    b. I prefer to come off as joyful and energetic.
    c. I'd rather come across as confident.
    d. I try my best to appear loving and compassionate.
    e. I want to seem expressive and outspoken.
    f. I want to be described as wise.
    g. I want people to associate me with a sense of connection.

3. Which of the following self-care activities do you tend to do the most?
    a. Eating healthy and balanced meals.
    b. Journaling.
    c. Spending time in nature.
    d. Exercising.
    e. Creative activities like drawing, writing, painting, etc.
    f. Tarot and oracle card pull.
    g. Meditation.
4. Do you often feel bored with the flow of life?
    a. Yes, I usually feel very bored with the way things are going.
    b. No, I'm very satisfied with the way things are.
5. Which gemstone are you most drawn to?
    a. Carnelian.
    b. Tiger's Eye.
    c. Amber.
    d. Rose Quartz.
    e. Blue Lace Agate.
    f. Sapphire.
    g. Amethyst.
6. Do you find honesty a challenging practice with both yourself and others?
    a. Yes, more often than not, honesty is burdensome.
    b. No, speaking my truth comes naturally to me.
7. Which of these flowers is your favorite?
    a. Roses
    b. Hibiscuses
    c. Sunflowers
    d. Pink phloxes
    e. Dandelions
    f. Purple Egyptian lotuses
    g. Pink lotuses

8. Do you usually find it hard to focus on certain tasks?
    a. Yes, I get distracted very easily.
    b. No, I can maintain a rather stable attention span until I finish the task at hand.

9. Which essential oil would you rather use at the moment?
    a. Frankincense essential oil.
    b. Orange essential oil.
    c. Lemon and ginger essential oils.
    d. Lavender essential oil.
    e. Peppermint essential oil.
    f. Sandalwood essential oil.
    g. Jasmine essential oil.

10. Do you have a hard time talking about your emotions?
    a. Yes, I usually don't know how to express my feelings. I try to avoid the subject because expressing my emotions weakens me.
    b. No, I have no trouble expressing my emotions and how I feel. I feel as though a huge burden is lifted off my chest.

11. Where would you rather be right now?
    a. Taking a long walk or hike through the forest.
    b. Overlooking Copacabana's majestic beaches.
    c. Visiting the great Giza Pyramids.
    d. Touring Barcelona's colorful Park Güell.
    e. Canoeing down Venice's river.
    f. Journeying through the Inca Trail to Machu Picchu with the llamas.
    g. Marveling at the beauty of the Taj Mahal.

12. Do you usually feel it's impossible to turn your life around and make positive changes?
    a. Yes, I tend to feel very powerless when it comes to making things happen. My life can't change overnight.

    b. No. I believe I am in charge of creating my own reality. I can bring my desires to life.

13. Close your eyes and bring your awareness to your body. Notice all your sensations and how your body feels. Relax and try to relieve all the tension. After taking a few moments to calm down, identify the area where you feel the most discomfort.

    a. The adrenal glands are right over the kidneys, kidneys, feet, or hips.

    b. You feel discomfort in the ovaries or have been struggling with hormonal imbalances lately.

    c. Your digestive system could receive a little attention.

    d. You've been experiencing lung issues; your blood circulation is rather unbalanced, your heartbeats are slower or faster than usual (or you have other heart problems), or you have a weak immune system.

    e. You have thyroid issues, your throat usually hurts, you have mouth, teeth, or jaw ailments, or you often experience an uncomfortable ringing in your ears.

    f. Your pituitary area hurts, you have eye problems, your sinuses are often blocked, or you struggle with frequent and severe headaches.

    g. The pineal gland area brings you the most discomfort. You may struggle with insomnia and your nerves, and you are naturally very anxious.

14. Do you usually find yourself avoiding others for fear of not being able to relate to them?

    a. Yes. I'm worried I won't be able to connect with others or understand them deeply.

    b. No. I'm generally empathetic, and I don't struggle with building intimate relationships with others.

15. Do you tend to overcompensate for your perceived inadequacies in other areas of your life? This can mean that you overwork yourself, overeat, over-exercise, overachieve, etc.

    a. Yes. I usually find myself going to great lengths to prove my success.

    b. Yes. I over-indulge in harmful habits as an escape.

c. No. I am confident in my abilities, and I'm keen on finding the right balance in all aspects of life.

16. Does the prospect of moving forward in life or committing to great changes frighten you?
    a. Yes. I hate going out of my comfort zone. I avoid surprises as much as I can.
    b. No. I am always very excited to take steps forward and see what the next big thing life has in store for me.

17. Do you accidentally (or intentionally) seek out relationships that are purely sexual or are based on physical attractiveness and appearance?
    a. Yes. I'm not looking for anything serious in a relationship. Having fun is my topmost priority.
    b. Yes. I don't know why I seem to attract sexual relationships even though I'm willing to commit.
    c. No. My relationships are meaningful. I always seek out partners I can truly connect with.

18. Are you easily angered, vexed, or irritated?
    a. Yes. The slightest inconveniences can set me off and ruin my entire day.
    b. No. I have a balanced temper and can take things lightly whenever I need to.

19. Do physical interactions and human touch make you feel uncomfortable and agitated?
    a. Yes. I don't like it when others touch me, even when it's a friendly gesture.
    b. No, I don't mind physical interactions.

20. Are you overly critical of the world and those around you?
    a. Yes. I usually find myself being critical of everything around me. I'm thinking about it even if I don't always voice it. It's something I can't really control.
    b. No. I believe I'm neither judgmental nor critical. What doesn't concern me doesn't vex me. I like to

think I'm easygoing.

21. Does your mood shift easily?

   a. Yes. I've gotten at least a few comments on how my mood rapidly shifts.

   b. No. I don't think I experience major shifts in my mood unless the situation truly warrants it.

22. Are you constantly tired, lethargic, or worn down?

   a. Yes. I feel very tired and out of energy most of the time.

   b. No. I'm very active and have no trouble getting many things done throughout the day.

Quiz Results

Questions 2, 3, 5, 7, 9, 11, and 13:

Count your answer as a point toward its correspondent chakra.

   a. Root Chakra

   b. Sacral Chakra

   c. Solar Plexus Chakra

   d. Heart Chakra

   e. Throat Chakra

   f. Third-Eye Chakra

   g. Crown Chakra

Chakra		Added Points	Deducted Points
Root Chakra	2, 3, 5, 7, 9, 11, 13	I	
Sacral Chakra	2, 3, 5, 7, 9, 11, 13	I	
Solar Plexus Chakra	2, 3, 5, 7, 9, 11, 13	IIII	

Heart Chakra	2, 3, 5, 7, 9, 11, 13	I	
Throat Chakra	2, 3, 5, 7, 9, 11, 13	-I -I	
Third-Eye Chakra	2, 3, 5, 7, 9, 11, 13	II	
Crown Chakra	2, 3, 5, 7, 9, 11, 13	III	

Question 1:

Deduct a point from the correspondent chakra.

    a. Root Chakra

    b. Sacral Chakra

    c. Solar Plexus Chakra

    d. Heart Chakra

    e. Throat Chakra

    f. Third-Eye Chakra

    g. Crown Chakra

Question 4:

    a. Deduct a point from the Crown Chakra

    b. Add a point to the Crown Chakra

Question 6:

    a. Deduct a point from the Throat Chakra

    b. Add a point to the Throat Chakra

Question 8:

    a. Deduct a point from the Root Chakra

    b. Add a point to the Root Chakra

Question 10:

    a. Deduct a point from the Heart Chakra

    b. Add a point to the Heart Chakra

Question 12:
    a. Deduct a point from the Third-Eye Chakra
    b. Add a point to the Third-Eye Chakra

Question 14:
    a. Deduct a point from the Sacral Chakra
    b. Add a point to the Sacral Chakra

Question 15:
    a. Deduct a point from your Crown Chakra
    b. Deduct a point from your Crown Chakra
    c. Add a point to your Crown Chakra

Question 16:
    a. Deduct a point from the Third-Eye Chakra
    b. Add a point to the Third-Eye Chakra

Question 17:
    a. Deduct a point from the Sacral Chakra
    b. Add a point to the Sacral Chakra

Question 18:
    a. Deduct a point from the Solar Plexus Chakra
    b. Add a point to the Solar Plexus Chakra

Question 19:
    a. Deduct a point from the Root Chakra
    b. Add a point to the Root Chakra

Question 20:
    a. Deduct a point from the Throat Chakra
    b. Add a point to the Throat Chakra

Question 21:
    a. Deduct a point from the Heart Chakra
    b. Add a point to the Heart Chakra

Question 22:
    a. Deduct a point from the Solar Plexus Chakra
    b. Add a point to the Solar Plexus Chakra

The chakra with the least number of points is unbalanced and needs healing.

Conclusion

When we open our chakras and partake in clearing and balancing them, our physical, mental, and spiritual being experiences a dramatic positive shift. Chakra healing practices optimize the function of the immune system and promote smooth blood flow throughout our body. This guarantees the health of our bodily organs and boosts our mental and cognitive function. When our chakras are aligned, we have better stress management and gain more control over our emotions. Our self-awareness, level of consciousness, and intuition are also refined. The chakra healing journey is an incredibly eye-opening one. It teaches us to identify and evaluate our emotions, thoughts, relationships, and life experiences at large. It gives us the strength to peacefully let go of all the things that no longer serve us to make room for better, more positive things.

As you already know, numerous internal and external factors can contribute to the obstruction of the chakras. While each chakra is associated with certain causes, our energy centers are generally blocked when negative emotions and thoughts overtake us. These feelings are bound to arise now and then. We are also susceptible to picking up negative energy from those around us. That said, how we deal with these situations and emotions can either help us maintain the free flow of energy throughout the body or cause them to fall out of balance.

Maintaining balance in the chakra system is a rigorous, constant effort. You can't decide to drop all your efforts once you feel a positive shift in your energy. This is because abandoning the positive activities you've picked up and going back to your old ways will lower your vibrational frequencies. When that happens, your chakras will fall out of balance and become obstructed, as if you hadn't done anything in the first place. For that reason, consistency is key to ensuring a steady flow of vital life force energy throughout your body. You need to start viewing your positive efforts and practices as a potential lifestyle rather than a temporary endeavor.

When our chakras are blocked, our quality of life drastically decreases. Managing and coping with numerous aspects of life can quickly become very challenging. The exact symptoms you experience will depend on the blocked energy center. The obstruction typically manifests as a physical, mental, or emotional issue.

Fortunately, there are many ways you can clear and re-balance your chakras. Throughout this insightful and knowledge-packed book, you learned all about how you can support each chakra with calibrated yoga poses. You better understand how certain yoga poses can help activate their correspondent chakra. By now, you should be able to determine which energy center a certain yoga pose can leave the most impact on. You also have insight into how you can use healing crystals to promote the activation of your chakras. You understand how to choose the right crystals for your needs and how to incorporate them into your yoga practice. If you wish to continue your chakra healing journey, you can explore more methods and techniques, such as reiki, sound healing, chakra massage therapy, essential oils for healing, and more!

Here's another book by Mari Silva that you might like

Your Free Gift
(only available for a limited time)

Thanks for getting this book! If you want to learn more about various spirituality topics, then join Mari Silva's community and get a free guided meditation MP3 for awakening your third eye. This guided meditation mp3 is designed to open and strengthen ones third eye so you can experience a higher state of consciousness. Simply visit the link below the image to get started.

https://spiritualityspot.com/meditation

References

Arora, I. (2010, December). Chakra Meditation with Mudra and Mantra. In International Symposium on YOGism.

Bhavanani, A. B., & Ramanathan, M. (2014). Meditation: the inner yoga. Souvenir of the CME on "Sleep, consciousness, and meditation: neurological correlates." Department of Physiology & CYTER, MGMCRI, Puducherry.

Chaturvedi, D. K., Arora, J. K., & Bhardwaj, R. (2015). Effect of meditation on chakra energy and hemodynamic parameters. International Journal of Computer Applications.

Dudeja, J. P. (2017). Scientific analysis of mantra-based meditation and its beneficial effects: An overview. International Journal of Advanced Scientific Technologies in Engineering and Management Sciences.

Fernros, L., Furhoff, A. K., & Wändell, P. E. (2008). Improving quality of life using compound mind-body therapies: evaluation of a course intervention with body movement and breath therapy, guided imagery, chakra experiencing, and mindfulness meditation. Quality of life research.

Goswami, S. S. (1999). Layayoga: The definitive guide to the chakras and kundalini. Simon and Schuster.

Johari, H. (2000). Chakras: Energy centers of transformation. Simon and Schuster.

Kim, T. S., Park, J. S., & Kim, M. A. (2008). The relation of meditation to power and well-being. Nursing Science Quarterly.

Lim, S., & Lee, H. (2020). Self-Exploration on Anxiety in Chakra Meditation Experienced People-The Mediation Effect of Emotional Health state Perception.

Poonia, S., & Gurjar, K. S. (2020). The effect of chakra meditation on heart chakra. Indian Journal of Physical Education, Sports Medicine & Exercise Science.

Rajalakshmi, M. C. (2019). Efficacy of Ajna Chakra Meditation in Primary Insomnia (Doctoral dissertation, Government Yoga and Naturopathy Medical College, Chennai).

Redmond, L. (2012). Chakra meditation: Transformation through the seven energy centers of the body. Sounds True.

Sanyal, K. Chakra Meditation and Five Elements Engagement of the Chakras with Five Elements in Nature. Role of Arts, Culture, Humanities, Religion, Education, Ethics, Philosophy, Spirituality and Science for Holistic Societal Development.

Viswanathan, P., & Pinto, N. (2015). The effects of classical music-based chakra meditation on the symptoms of premenstrual syndrome. Int J Indian Psychology

Yoga and Spirituality. (n.d.). Art Of Living (India). https://www.artofliving.org/in-en/yoga/yoga-benefits/yoga-and-spirituality

Rohan, E. (2022, May 20). Today's menopause solutions Aren't your mom's hot-flash remedies (I know because I asked mine). Well+Good. https://www.wellandgood.com/menopause-solutions-phenology/

zaleska. (2021, November 24). What chakras are and how yoga can help balance them. Cleveland Clinic. https://health.clevelandclinic.org/chakras/

21 yoga myths and misconceptions explained. (2022, March 21). Origympersonaltrainercourses.Co.Uk.

All about yoga: 15 health benefits. (n.d.). EMedicineHealth. https://www.emedicinehealth.com/yoga/article_em.htm

Carrico, M., Pacheco, R., Radcliffe, S., Chen, J., & Wolff, M. (2007, August 28). Meditation for beginners: How to meditate, its benefits, & methods. Yoga Journal. https://www.yogajournal.com/meditation/how-to-meditate/let-s-meditate/

Chakra yoga explained – A full guide to the 7 Chakras. (2020, July 13). TINT Yoga. https://tintyoga.com/magazine/chakra-yoga/

ChopraTM, D. (2016, April 21). 3 ways you can benefit from your chakras. Chopra. https://chopra.com/articles/3-ways-you-can-benefit-from-your-chakras

Clarke, A. (2021, October 13). 7 most popular types of yoga. Livescience.Com; Live Science. https://www.livescience.com/7-types-of-yoga

ET Bureau. (2016, June 17). Here are 10 myths about yoga debunked. Economic Times. https://economictimes.indiatimes.com/magazines/panache/here-are-10-myths-about-yoga-debunked/articleshow/52790951.cms

Haigh, C. (2013, September 12). 7 reasons you should start doing yoga immediately. Lifehack. https://www.lifehack.org/articles/lifestyle/7-reasons-you-should-start-doing-yoga-immediately.html

Halse, H. (2011, January 27). Kundalini yoga vs. Hatha yoga. LIVESTRONG.COM. https://www.livestrong.com/article/366636-kundalini-yoga-vs-hatha-yoga/

Haney, C. (2019, February 15). Yoga for beginners: 7 tips for starting yoga for the first time. JadeYoga. https://jadeyoga.com/blogs/news/yoga-for-beginners-7-tips-for-starting-yoga-for-the-first-time

Jha, B. (2019, July 16). Types of yoga: 7 true traditional styles of yoga. IndianYug. https://indianyug.com/types-of-yoga/

Lizzy. (2014, October 21). How to use yoga poses to awaken your chakras. Chakras.Info. https://www.chakras.info/chakra-yoga/

McGee, K. (2020, May 12). 11 types of yoga: A breakdown of the major styles. Mindbodygreen. https://www.mindbodygreen.com/articles/the-11-major-types-of-yoga-explained-simply

MEA. (n.d.). Ministry of External Affairs, Government of India. https://www.mea.gov.in/search-result.htm?25096/Yoga:_su_origen,_historia_y_desarrollo

Mhel. (2019, September 2). How is Kundalini Different from Hatha/Vinyasa? Read This. Brett Larkin Yoga. https://www.brettlarkin.com/kundalini-yoga-different-hathavinyasa/

Nichols, H. (2021, March 25). Yoga: Methods, types, philosophy, and risks. Medicalnewstoday.Com. https://www.medicalnewstoday.com/articles/286745

Paul Jerard, E.-R. (2010, March 9). The seven chakra system of Hatha Yoga. Yoga Teacher Training Blog. https://www.yoga-teacher-training.org/2010/03/09/the-seven-chakra-system-of-hatha-yoga/

Pizer, A. (n.d.). What is an Asana in Yoga? Verywell Fit. https://www.verywellfit.com/what-is-asana-3566793

Regan, S. (2021, May 18). 15 signs you're having A Kundalini awakening + what it means. Mindbodygreen. https://www.mindbodygreen.com/articles/kundalini-awakening

Rodrigues, S. (2014, August 17). The 7 true traditional types of Yoga. FitBodyHQ. http://www.fitbodyhq.com/yoga/7-true-traditional-types-yoga/

Saal, K. (2021, February 9). What is Asana in yoga. One Flow Yoga. https://oneflowyoga.com/blog/asana-yoga

Tran, P. (2019, May 21). Yoga & meditation. EverydayYoga.Com. https://www.everydayyoga.com/blogs/guides/yoga-meditation

Understanding the chakras and Kundalini energy. (n.d.). Art Of Living (Global). https://www.artofliving.org/wisdom/theme/kundalini-and-chakras

Vinyasa. (n.d.). Yogapedia.Com https://www.yogapedia.com/definition/5035/vinyasa

Walsh, S. (2019, August 22). 7 yoga poses to balance your chakras. Mindbodygreen. https://www.mindbodygreen.com/0-11865/7-yoga-poses-to-balance-your-chakras.html

What is pranayama? (2014, August 6). Ekhart Yoga. https://www.ekhartyoga.com/articles/practice/what-is-pranayama

What is Yoga? Sadhguru dispels 3 misconceptions about Yoga. (n.d.). Sadhguru.Org. https://isha.sadhguru.org/yoga/new-to-yoga/what-is-yoga/

Winters, E. R., Schettler, R. M., Asp, K., Turner, L., The Clean Eating Team, & Adams, H. (2010, December 14). 5 biggest misconceptions about yoga. Yoga Journal. https://www.yogajournal.com/lifestyle/5-biggest-misconceptions-about-yoga/

Yoga. (n.d.). Yogapedia.Com. https://www.yogapedia.com/definition/4/yoga

Yoga and pranayama - A yogic breathing exercise. (n.d.). Art Of Living (Global). https://www.artofliving.org/yoga/breathing-techniques/yoga-and-pranayama

Yoga to balance and open up chakras. (n.d.). Art Of Living (Global https://www.artofliving.org/yoga-balance-and-open-chakras

Yoga: What you need to know. (n.d.). NCCIH. https://www.nccih.nih.gov/health/yoga-what-you-need-to-know

zaleska. (2021, November 24). What chakras are and how yoga can help balance them. Cleveland Clinic. https://health.clevelandclinic.org/chakras/

(N.d.). Yogabasics.Com https://www.yogabasics.com/practice/yoga-for-beginners/yoga-tips-for-beginners/

Raquel. (2020, May 2). 9 Ways to Make Yoga a Daily Habit (that will stick). Prettyeasylife.Com. https://www.prettyeasylife.com/9-ways-to-make-yoga-a-daily-habit-that-will-stick/

Drollinger, J. (2021). Root chakra: Activating, balancing, and healing: Mind body and soul connection. Independently Published.

Onyx Team. (2020, May 3). Root Chakra Healing: Everything you Need to Know. Onyx Integrative Medicine & Aesthetics.

https://onyxintegrative.com/root-chakra-healing/

/shahparita. (2019, June 22). 9 signs your Root Chakra energy is grounded. YogiApprovedTM. https://www.yogiapproved.com/grounded-root-chakra/

The Root Chakra: Your personal guide to balance the first chakra. (n.d.). Art Of Living (United States).

Yoga sequence for root chakra (Muladhara). (n.d.). Tummee.Com. https://www.tummee.com/yoga-sequences/yoga-sequence-for-root-muladhara-chakra

Dadabhay, Y. (2021, November 25). 11 amazing sacral chakra opening symptoms. Subconscious Servant. https://subconsciousservant.com/sacral-chakra-opening-symptoms/

Editors, Y. J., Indries, M., Marglin, A. T. to, & LaRue, M. B. (2021, April 27). What you need to know about the sacral chakra. Yoga Journal. https://www.yogajournal.com/yoga-101/intro-sacral-chakra-svadhisthana/

Jain, R. (2020, August 26). Svadhishthana - Sacral Chakra: All you need to know. Arhanta Yoga Ashrams. https://www.arhantayoga.org/blog/svadhishthana-chakra-all-you-need-to-know-about-the-sacral-chakra/

Oils, R. M. (n.d.). Exploring your sacral chakra. Rockymountainoils.Com. https://www.rockymountainoils.com/learn/exploring-your-sacral-chakra/

Sacral chakra. (n.d.). Anahana.Com. https://www.anahana.com/en/yoga/sacral-chakra

Shah, P. (2019, September 2). Getting your sacral chakra back in balance. THE FULLEST. https://thefullest.com/2019/09/02/getting-your-sacral-chakra-back-in-balance/

Want to deepen your sensuality? Look to the sacral chakra. (2021, December 6). Healthline. https://www.healthline.com/health/mind-body/sacral-chakra

Yoga Bear. (2017, July 30). Balance your sacral chakra with these yoga poses. RTÉ. https://www.rte.ie/lifestyle/living/2017/0727/893438-balance-your-sacral-chakra-with-these-yoga-poses/

yoga/, /hannahleatherbury. (2018, August 25). 5 Yoga Practices For Balancing the Solar Plexus Chakra. YogiApprovedTM. https://www.yogiapproved.com/solar-plexus-chakra-healing/

Ribas, S. (2019, April 26). How To Balance Your Solar Plexus Chakra. The Yoga Collective. https://www.theyogacollective.com/how-to-balance-your-solar-plexus-chakra/

Dadabhay, Y. (2021, September 29). 11 Signs You Have A Blocked Solar Plexus Chakra. Subconscious Servant. https://subconsciousservant.com/blocked-solar-plexus-chakra/

Solar Plexus Chakra. (n.d.). Anahana.Com. https://www.anahana.com/en/yoga/solar-plexus-chakra

Oils, R. M. (n.d.). Exploring Your Solar Plexus Chakra. Rockymountainoils.Com. https://www.rockymountainoils.com/learn/exploring-your-solar-plexus-chakra/

Signs Your Solar Plexus Chakra is Opening. (n.d.). Kelleemaize.Com https://www.kelleemaize.com/post/signs-your-solar-plexus-chakra-is-opening

5 best heart chakra yoga poses for compassion & understanding. (2020, September 18). Taylor's Tracks. https://www.taylorstracks.com/heart-chakra-yoga-poses/

5 yoga poses that activate anahata - the heart chakra. (n.d.). SELF-ELEVATION.COM

alissalastres. (2018, April 25). Crack your heart open with these 7 heart opening yoga poses. YogiApprovedTM. https://www.yogiapproved.com/7-yoga-poses-to-open-your-heart/

Blocked heart chakra: Fixing the imbalance in your chakra system. (2020, November 26). BetterMe Blog. https://betterme.world/articles/blocked-heart-chakra/

Charlotte. (2022, March 31). 15 major heart chakra opening symptoms for a happier life. Typically, Topical. https://typicallytopical.com/heart-chakra-opening-symptoms/

Dadabhay, Y. (2020, September 29). 11 symptoms of your heart chakra opening. Subconscious Servant. https://subconsciousservant.com/heart-chakra-opening-symptoms/

Editors, Y. J., Indries, M., Marglin, A. T. to, & LaRue, M. B. (2021, March 12). Everything you need to know about the heart chakra. Yoga Journal. https://www.yogajournal.com/yoga-101/chakras-yoga-for-beginners/intro-heart-chakra-anahata/

Five asanas to stimulate the heart chakra. (2020, August 6). BALANCE. https://balance.media/heart-chakra-asanas/

Kandanarachchi, P. (2013). Heart Chakra. Lulu.com. https://www.anahana.com/en/yoga/heart-chakra

Katie. (2017, March 19). Follow your heart: How to spot an imbalance in your heart chakra. MoreYoga. https://www.moreyoga.co.uk/follow-your-heart-how-to-spot-an-imbalance-in-your-heart-chakra/

Kristin. (2021, February 10). Heart chakra: Everything you need to know. Be My Travel Muse. https://www.bemytravelmuse.com/heart-chakra/

Parpworth-Reynolds, C. (2020, October 30). 11 signs of A blocked heart chakra. Subconscious Servant. https://subconsciousservant.com/heart-chakra-blockage-symptoms/

Ready for bold self-love? Try these 4 tone ups for the heart chakra. (2019, July 7). Mindbodygreen. https://www.mindbodygreen.com/articles/hearth-chakra-healing-4-exercises-to-open-a-blocked-chakra/

Robledo, G. (2021, June 13). 12 heart chakra blockage signs & symptoms. Making Mindfulness Fun. https://www.makingmindfulnessfun.com/heart-chakra-blockage-symptoms/

Salamba Bhujangasana. (n.d.). Yogapedia.Com. https://www.yogapedia.com/definition/7048/salamba-bhujangasana

Seventh Wonder. (2018, June 9). Understanding your heart, Chakra. Seventh-Wonder.Com. https://seventh-wonder.com/understanding-your-heart-chakra/

Steber, C., & Ferraro, K. (2018, February 1). 15 signs your heart chakra is blocked. Bustle. https://www.bustle.com/wellness/signs-your-heart-chakra-is-blocked-its-messing-with-your-love-life

Team SEEMA. (2021, November 14). Everything to know about The Green heart chakra. Seema. https://www.seema.com/everything-to-know-about-the-green-heart-chakra/

The Heart Chakra: Discover and balance the fourth chakra. (n.d.). Art Of Living (United States).

Warrior Pose I. (n.d.). Tummee.Com. https://www.tummee.com/yoga-poses/warrior-pose-i

(N.d.). Yogainternational.Com https://yogainternational.com/article/view/a-heart-opening-sequence-for-natarajasana-king-dancer-pose

rashmi. (2020, May 21). 12 Yoga Poses For Throat Chakra To Discover Your Voice And Confidence. Yogarsutra. https://www.yogarsutra.com/yoga-poses-throat-chakra/11

Throat Chakra Opening Symptoms. (n.d.). Abundance No Limits. https://www.abundancenolimits.com/throat-chakra-opening-symptoms/

Snyder, S., Editors, Y. J., Indries, M., Marglin, A. T. to, & LaRue, M. B. (2021, July 30). Everything You Need to Know About the Throat Chakra. Yoga Journal. https://www.yogajournal.com/yoga-101/chakras-yoga-for-beginners/chakratuneup2015-intro-visuddha/

Throat Chakra. (n.d.). Anahana.Com. https://www.anahana.com/en/yoga/throat-chakra

Singh, J. (2019, August 16). Seven Signs of Throat (Vishuddha) Chakra Blockage. JagjotSingh. https://jagjotsingh.com/throat-chakra-blockage/

Kristin. (2021, February 13). Third eye chakra: Everything you need to know. Be My Travel Muse. https://www.bemytravelmuse.com/third-eye-chakra/

McCarthy, K. (2020, July 2). 10 yoga poses to open your third eye chakra. TheThings. https://www.thethings.com/yoga-poses-open-third-eye-chakra/

Stokes, V. (2021, May 6). How to open your third eye chakra for spiritual awakening. Healthline. https://www.healthline.com/health/mind-body/how-to-open-your-third-eye

Team SEEMA. (2021, September 23). The beginner's guide to the third eye chakra. Seema. https://www.seema.com/the-beginners-guide-to-the-third-eye-chakra/

The Third Eye Chakra: Discover and balance the sixth chakra. (n.d.). Art Of Living (United States).

Third eye chakra or Ajna chakra. (2021, August 5). Ekhart Yoga. https://www.ekhartyoga.com/articles/practice/third-eye-chakra-ajna-chakra

Third Eye Chakra stones: 15 must-have crystals for the Ajna. (n.d.). Tiny Rituals. https://tinyrituals.co/blogs/tiny-rituals/third-eye-chakra-stones

5 signs your crown chakra is blocked or weak. (n.d.). Your Sanctuary For Healing. http://www.yoursanctuaryforhealing.com/blog/5-signs-your-crown-chakra-is-blocked-or-weak

8 Yoga Poses For Your Crown Chakra. (n.d.). Kelleemaize.Com. https://www.kelleemaize.com/post/8-yoga-poses-for-your-crown-chakra

Behind the meaning. (n.d.). Daisy London. https://www.daisyjewellery.com/blogs/our-world/behind-the-meaning-the-crown-chakra

Cameron, Y. (2022, Februar2y 7). An introduction to the crown chakra + how to heal it. Mindbodygreen. https://www.mindbodygreen.com/0-92/Crown-Chakra-Healing-Opening-For-Beginners.html

Crocodile Pose (Makarasana). (n.d.). Art Of Living (United States) https://www.artofliving.org/us-en/crocodile-pose-makarasana

Crown chakra. (n.d.). Anahana.Com https://www.anahana.com/en/yoga/crown-chakra

Ezrin, S., Husler, A., & Land, R. (2021, December 14). Lotus Pose. Yoga Journal. https://www.yogajournal.com/poses/lotus-pose/